Capitalism's New Clothes

Capitalism's New Clothes

Enterprise, Ethics and Enjoyment in Times of Crisis

COLIN CREMIN

PlutoPress
www.plutobooks.com

First published 2011 by Pluto Press
345 Archway Road, London N6 5AA

www.plutobooks.com

Distributed in the United States of America exclusively by
Palgrave Macmillan, a division of St. Martin's Press LLC,

British Library Cataloguing in Publication Data
A catalogue record for this book is available from the British Library

ISBN   978 0 7453 2815 7   Hardback
ISBN   978 0 7453 2814 0   Paperback

Library of Congress Cataloging in Publication Data applied for

10   9   8   7   6   5   4   3   2   1

Designed and produced for Pluto Press by Chase Publishing Services Ltd
Typeset from disk by Stanford DTP Services, Northampton, England
Simultaneously printed digitally by CPI Antony Rowe, Chippenham, UK
and Edwards Bros in the USA

CONTENTS

ACKNOWLEDGEMENTS

First of all, my immense gratitude to all of the people at Pluto Press, and especially David Castle, for their support in helping me to realise this first book project. Thanks also to the anonymous reviewers and the editors of journal articles cited in the book. In New Zealand, I would like to thank the staff (academic and administrative) from the Department of Sociology at the University of Auckland for helping create such a pleasant working environment. Special mention goes to Bruce Curtis and Tracey McIntosh who have been especially supportive in their roles as heads of department; and Steve Matthewman whose comments on drafts have proven invaluable. I am also grateful to Alyssa Lee for helping to gather material for the ecology chapter and the Faculty of Arts at the University of Auckland for funding her Summer Scholarship. Thanks, too, to the students taking my courses at Auckland: their enthusiasm, intellect and imagination make teaching both a privilege and a pleasure. Thanks to Eluned Summers-Bremner for all her help and support in helping me to secure a grant for a related project. Also, my gratitude to Sarah Thompson for the initial proofreading of the book and Nuala Ernest for the final copy-editing.

Beyond Auckland, I would like to thank my PhD supervisors, first, Richard Kilminster for having confidence in me during the most trying of times and for his ongoing support and encouragement, and Ray Pawson who was also instrumental in helping me through the more difficult periods of my study. Thanks also to colleagues and friends at Sunderland University where I previously worked. Carole Wright, Austin Harrington and Greg Martin whose friendships I value on many levels, and Julie Lord who continues to inspires me in thought and in practice. Special thanks to John M. Roberts for encouraging me through the difficult moments while also proving to be an invaluable critic and mine of information. Finally, to the people not specifically mentioned here who over the years have given their time, friendship and love along this sometimes hazardous journey, I thank you all.

1

INTRODUCTION

The story of the Emperor's New Clothes is one we are all familiar with. It is often used as a metaphor for ideology. Capitalism is the naked emperor and the new clothes whatever ideological gown we drape over him to forget or disavow what is only too apparent. Ideology is our reality. It enables us to make sense out of non-sense, to have a sense of who we are and to generate meaning from chaos. When, in 2008, the financial markets went into turmoil, even the most skilled of tailors had trouble convincing anyone that the Emperor was anything but naked. Everybody could hear the little boy shouting, 'Look, the Emperor isn't wearing any clothes!' and in every quarter the media pundits, the free-market evangelists and the politicians all scrambled around hopelessly trying to find a way to cover the embarrassment. The corrupt financial traders, profligate consumers, inept politicians, eventually even the public sector, were the targets of ire stitched together to form a ragtag garment of ideological indeterminacy. We all had to pitch in to get through a crisis we were all somehow made to be responsible for. But what kind of capitalism are we speaking of here?

There are many ways to clothe what is essentially a system based on the perpetual exploitation of all resources, human and natural, for the purposes of profit or what Marx called surplus-value. Sometimes the fabric is of a racist or sexist nature. The Emperor's finest tailors, the corporations, liberal-parliamentary state, non-governmental organisations (NGOs) and so on, are not in the habit of using such yarns although their practices often suggest otherwise. Theirs are more refined and softer on the eyes. This book is about an ideology woven by the enterprise of those concerned about the ethics of capitalism and at the same time embarrassed by the enjoyments the system has afforded them.

From a linguistic perspective we can never escape ideology. We might see through certain layers, but eventually we have to account for the nakedness through the imprecise device of language. In talking about capitalism's new clothes we draw attention to the fact that, however the social relations of society are dressed, there are truths about those relations that make some interpretations better than others. Critical theorists engage in an endless quest for that truth. Some of the best have shown that by combining the materialism of Marx, psychoanalytic theory and social linguistics, you have a better prospect of unpicking the threads of the social relations, subjective desires and ideological props than those who employ one approach at the expense of the others. Postmodern theory, with its emphasis on linguistics, is a case in point. So too, though, is the cruder materialism of the dogmatic versions of Marxism. Some of the most impressive theorists, such as Adorno, Marcuse, Deleuze, Žižek and Badiou, have often been accused of under-theorising or misappropriating Marx. The more serious problems lie with those that in Chapter 2 I describe as left-liberals. I am thinking here of figures such as Michael Hardt and Toni Negri, Ulrich Beck, John Urry and others who while critical of many aspects of capitalism tend, in my view, to confuse rather than advance analysis on the fundamentals.

Marxists sometimes neglect the buried impulses of subjectivity and the ideological knots into which we are all linguistically bound. In the past 30 or so years, many disillusioned Marxists have neglected political economy. *Capitalism's New Clothes* subscribes to a form of ideological critique that makes use of materialist, linguistic and psychoanalytic concepts to theorise the individual and society at this critical juncture. It explores, in the tradition of critical theory, the ideological configurations of apparatuses of power and how they are reproduced and challenged at a subjective level in societies oriented to mass consumption. It borrows from and advances observations of Frankfurt School theorists, such as Theodor Adorno and Herbert Marcuse, who describe how people are seduced into wanting a system that essentially enslaves them.

It returns to progenitors, Marx, Weber and Freud, while looking to more contemporary theorists such as Slavoj Žižek, whose advocacy of a 'politics of the impossible' this book endorses.

Herbert Marcuse wrote of a one-dimensional man who finds happiness in the superficial pleasures of consumption. Christopher Lasch described a culture of narcissism in which people identify in others a reflection of their own egos. Zygmunt Bauman read into processes of de-industrialisation and class fragmentation a liquid modernity characterised by fluid identities and loss of social bearing. *Capitalism's New Clothes* follows in this tradition while also rejecting the dominant view in sociology today that Marx's key insights on political economy are either irrelevant or in need of complete overhaul. It recognises that capitalism is a dynamic system in which nation states and institutions play a supporting role in ensuring that private capital can extract surplus profit from property-less workers. While the fundamentals remain the same, it acknowledges important socio-economic changes which spill over into and reconfigure the public domain, affect social reproduction and cause changes in subjective constitution and ideological orientation.

The twin crises of economy and ecology present us with the objective limits of a system that depends for its existence on the unrelenting exploitation of all resources, ecology, material and mental labour and everything that people, in their unique ways, create. It seems that however objectively critical the tendencies of capitalism, or certain that it is human activity that causes global warming, or, from another angle, how ineffectual the individual as an atomised being is in responding to such seemingly intractable problems, life goes on pretty much as it has for most of our lives. We seem to be hurtling towards the abyss and, in the words of a large fast food chain, lovin' it.

Capitalism's New Clothes centres on three fundamental points. First, that we are not in liquid modernity, reflexive modernity, a new economy or risk society, the sort of new clothes commonly used to define capitalism today. Second, that ideologically, capitalism more than ever reveals itself as a system prone to repeated and intensifying crises that negatively and profoundly affect human life in its social and natural environment. Third, that we know there is a major crisis of capitalism, that there are extreme inequalities of wealth and power, that a majority of the world's population is in poverty, that violence and injustice everywhere prevail and, perhaps even more importantly, that the mode of production which threatens the ecosystem on which we all depend does not appear to pose a threat to the system and its chief beneficiaries. It is a naked capitalism that reveals itself for what it is, without, so far at least, its power diminishing. There are metaphorical little boys and girls, though not nearly enough of them.

The book is organised around three core themes: ideologies, actions, ethical values (enterprise, ethics and enjoyment), each with specific chapters that imbricate and iterate one another to conceptualise a 'one-dimensional society' for the twenty-first century. For the purposes of *Capitalism's New Clothes*, enterprise is taken to refer to the instrumental-calculative activities that drive capitalism forward and that Max Weber argued increasingly colour social action. The old coat of enterprise was brushed up in the 1980s and mass produced for a new enterprising culture. While fashions change, enterprise is a classic design popular to this day with added frills such as ethical and ecological enterprise. So, in the chapter on enterprise, I focus on enterprise as a subjective endeavour to gain competitive advantage on the labour market which shifts the signifier from enterprise to the more ambiguous, softer sounding, notion of employability. Ethics refers to concerns about the welfare of others and commitments to principles of equality and social justice, the sort of principled commitments that Max Weber called value-rational action. So in the chapter on ethics I focus on the way principles, often associated with the political left, are appropriated into and coordinated around the interests of capital. Enjoyment is used in a general sense to refer to subjective forms of pleasure, fun, play, excitement and so on. So, in the chapter on enjoyment, I explore the way activities associated with these terms are commodified. The analysis builds on the Frankfurt School critiques of consumer society and develops Lacan's point that today we are obliged to enjoy.

Enterprise, ethics and enjoyment are also described as injunctions. We must be enterprising by striving to possess objects that improve employability. We must be ethical by striving to improve the lives of others, the health of society and the planet. We must enjoy the pleasures of modern life and in doing so not take life so seriously as to become fixated on a particular labour or political cause. Enterprise, ethics and enjoyment come together – for example, when we get involved in campaigns to raise money for social causes through events such as pop concerts or activities such as fun runs. The arguments are developed using illustrative examples of this configuration, one that Herbert Marcuse had earlier noticed when he said that,

> In the sale of equipment for relaxing entertainment in bomb shelters, in the television show of competing candidates for national leadership, the juncture between politics, business, and fun is complete. But the juncture is fraudulent and fatally premature – business and fun are still the politics of domination. This is not a satire-play after the tragedy; it is not *finis tragoediae* – the tragedy may just begin. And again, it will not be the hero but the people who will be the ritual victims. (2002:106)

Approaching ideology through these three separate and synthetic injunctions allows for a richer interpretation into how capitalism as a naked form of exploitation is depoliticised. In regard to ethico-political causes, enterprise situates action within capitalism's ideologico-material matrix while enjoyment enters into every relationship, in the workplace, politics and of course consumption.

The three chapters are bookended with discussions on economy and ecology. The first provides the background of the analysis while the last adapts arguments from previous chapters for a critique of what is referred to here as the climate change industry. It is important to begin with the economy for a book that is indebted to critical theory. This component is the most under-theorised within the tradition I am most sympathetic to. The chapter makes some attempt, admittedly limited, to situate the arguments within a Marxism that subscribes to the labour theory of value without neglecting the complicated effects of desire and language on the capacity of workers to mount an effective challenge against capitalism. Scholars of Marx, or for that matter Lacan, will no doubt find shortcomings in the way concepts are appropriated. Sacrifices are made and liberties are taken with the theories used, but the end result hopefully justifies the means.

The economic and ecological problems we face are the metacrises of our times and perhaps of all times, so it is apt for a book that includes crisis in its title that these figure prominently here. These crises (material and ideological) are likely to intensify and by the time the book goes to print the warned of 'double-dip' recession could well be in full swing. If today the outlook does look bleak, then more than ever we need to examine the way the material economy, subjective desire and ideology imbricate one another so as to find ways in these configurations to prevent the future being written for us.

2

NAKED ECONOMY

The global financial crisis of 2008 put paid to the notion, at least rhetorically, that the market is the only game in town. Of course, the market never was the only game in town. Finance capital may have gone wild, but it was the state that forged a global framework that allowed this. This fact has not prevented some from claiming that the state has become a 'decentred' bit player in the global economy. This chapter is about neo-liberalism as an ideological project; it is about unsubstantiated assertions regarding the nature of society today; it is about where we are now and where we might be going. This is not a naked economy in the respect that non-economic factors play no role in tempering exchange relations; rather it is naked in that we are describing a society in which responses to the squeeze on surplus-value have been such a driving force for socio-economic change. The 'base' remains the very relations between capital and labour that Marx so eloquently described; however, it is through the 'superstructure' – institutions, ideology, and so on – that we make sense of the configurations that the mode of production depends on and identify here the dialectical tension between base and superstructure that Marx described. *Naked economy* provides a foreground for later chapters on how we are locked into a system that thrives on inequality, exploitation, alienation and violence.

The Stupid ID

If capitalism were conceived in Freudian terms, the unconscious raw energy or human drives called the id would be the market itself. The internalised superego authority would be the institutional frameworks that support and regulate it. The conscious ego would be the individuals, capitalists and workers, responding to the two opposing demands of id and superego. By renouncing its authority, the superego/state staged a retreat from the id creating a space for the stupid drives to wreak havoc. As the author of *The Great Transformation,* Karl Polanyi (1957) observed, if it was not for the state creating and regulating the legal frameworks that allowed for the commodification of land, labour and money, capitalism would not exist. There never is, nor could there be, an id without a superego to socialise it; to promote a neo-liberalism which Saad-Filho describes as,

> [A]n accumulation strategy, a mode of social and economic reproduction and a mode of exploitation and social domination based on the systematic use of state power to impose, under the ideological veil of non-intervention, a hegemonic project of recomposition of the rule of capital in all areas of social life. (2005:342)

In contrast to classical liberalism, which held that states and markets should be separated, the neo-liberal doctrine saw states and other institutions as functions of the market. According to this view, governments were incapable of predicting and adapting in time to shifts in consumer trends. State-owned industries, welfare systems, trade unions and protectionist economic policy undermined competitive efficiency either by propping up vested interests or removing incentives for businesses and people to adapt to changing market demands. According to the efficient market hypothesis, the state's role should be limited to providing a stable environment for businesses to compete in. This would also involve the creation of artificial markets where infrastructures prohibit competitive duplication, for example water supply, the railways and the electricity grid. Such examples illustrate the point made by David Harvey (2005a) and others[1] that the state is instrumental to neo-liberalism to the extent that it is accurate to say there is no such thing as laissez-faire.

Neo-liberalism is an ideological project that aims to open up the economy to competitive practices through deregulation, especially of finance, and privatisation of state assets and, crucially, to fashion people as atomised, self-aggrandising rational actors. Whereas Freud saw human subjectivity as the outcome of an act of self-sacrifice to wider social interests, this thesis held that people are in effect self-interested psychopaths (those promoting this thesis no doubt recognised such traits in themselves). And psychopaths, when free to pursue their own interests, act in the interests of capital because their very existence depends on the health of the companies they work for, or so it goes. Consequently, the worker has a vested interest in developing the skills, knowledge and personal attributes that business wants. The state, in turn, modelled legislation around this limited view of human subjectivity by making it harder for people to draw on welfare and easier for businesses to fire workers who were no longer able to meet their needs. In the Foucauldian reading, free-markets are a governing technology of power and, as Jose Gabriel Palma (2009) explains, life becomes the art of practising the principles of free-markets: the worker who seeks improvements by measuring his life against the standard of market competition becomes a docile body of neo-liberal discourse.

This ideology became a global orthodoxy with the help of state-backed institutions such as the World Bank, International Monetary Fund (IMF) and World Trade Organization (WTO). Developing countries were forced to open up their markets to foreign capital, remove state subsidies and introduce free-market reform into vulnerable sectors of the economy while privatising state institutions and industries. 'Shock therapy' was the preferred name for sabotaging the economies of the former Soviet bloc. This included a programme of rapid privatisation of all state assets and the introduction of competitive markets that, according to David Harvey (2005b), signalled a return to a smash and grab primitive accumulation or accumulation by dispossession. This mode of accumulation enacted on a global scale included the commodification and privatisation of land and national resources – state-owned industry and intellectual property – the suppression of rights over the commons including the forced expulsion of people from land to make way for agribusiness, the slave trade, monetisation of taxation and exchange. This was to accelerate the proletarianisation of labour and the growth of 'informal' sectors of the economy in the expanding slum areas of the world where 'entrepreneurialism' becomes a means for survival. Capitalism, Alex Callinicos (2007) explains, unifies under a global world system that ensures an extremely unequal geographical distribution of resources through restrictions on access to investments and markets with egregious effects on much of the world's population. Mike Davis provides an illustration of the impact of market reform at the micro-level of society. This from an aid worker in Haiti,

> Now everything is for sale. The woman used to receive you with hospitality, give you a coffee, share all that she had in her home. I could go get a plate of food at a neighbour's house; a child could get a coconut at her grandmother's, two mangoes at another aunt's. But these acts of solidarity are disappearing with the growth of poverty. Now when you arrive somewhere, either the woman offers to sell you a cup of coffee or she has no coffee at all. The tradition of mutual giving that allowed us to help each other and survive – this is all being lost. (Cited in Davis 2006:184)

Neo-liberalism is a multiplier. It multiplies the wealth of the few at the top and the numbers of people in poverty at the bottom, many who reside in the urban slums of major cities. In total, a staggering third of the world's population is estimated to live in slum dwellings (Davis 2006:23). Growing levels of inequality is a phenomenon of the more developed nations too. Between 1979 and 2006, the share the national income of the richest 1 per cent of the US population went up from 8.9 per cent to 22.8 per cent while, in real terms, the average national income of the bottom 90 per cent fell (Palma 2009:837). In 1979, 5 million households in the UK were on an income that was less than half the national average. By 1991–92 this had increased to 13.9 million, representing a rise from 9 per cent to 25 per cent of the population (Turner 2008:145). According to the Institute of Fiscal Studies, levels of inequality in the UK are today higher than at any time since records began in 1961 (Elliott 2008).[2]

The availability of cheap credit to increasingly indebted workers offset effects that a low wage economy would otherwise have had on consumer spending. By the end of January 2009, the total of UK personal debt stood at £1,457 billion (Credit Action 2010). In the US, between 1997 and 2007, total personal debt had increased from $5,547.1 billion to $14,374.5 billion, a rise of 159.1 per cent (Turner 2008). For comparison, David Harvey (2005a) reports that the total debt of the 60 poorest nations is $523 billion.

The flooding of credit into an overstretched market has been traced to the expansion of finance capital in the 1990s. This was facilitated by China, which had built up huge quantities of US dollar reserves used to purchase US bonds and securities or dollar-denominated assets (see Bello 2010). Giovanni Arrighi described financialisation as a method for generating profit from financial circulation rather than trade and commodity production. As Arrighi (2009:8) pointed out, intensification of competition between capitals makes investments in industrial capital, where the returns are not immediate, a riskier proposition given the amount of investments required. This leads to an accumulation of liquidity that, with the help of China, created the supply conditions for finance capital to expand. The point echoes Braudel's claim that financial expansion which happens at the expense of labour-intensive industrial investment, announces the autumn of a hegemonic system.

Fredric Jameson describes finance as, '[A] play of monetary entities which needs neither production (as capital does) nor consumption (as money does): which supremely, like cyberspace, can live on its own internal metabolism and circulate without any reference to an older type of content.' (1998:161) The problem is that sooner or later the real economy has to catch up with the fictitious one. While finance has expanded, the rates of economic growth have been in decline in the US for over half a century. Between 1950 and 1959, growth stood at 4.11 per cent. This dropped to 3.24 per cent in the 1970s and by the 1990s was a mere 3 per cent (The National Accounting Framework, cited in Saad-Filho & Johnston 2005:16).[3] In 1950, finance contributed 10 per cent to gross domestic product (GDP). By 2001, the figure stood at under 25 per cent while in the same period employment in finance had risen by just 3 per cent (Krippner 2005:189).

What these figures show is that neo-liberalism has been spectacularly unsuccessful in stimulating economic growth, increasing general levels of prosperity and creating a stable material-industrial foundation for work and investment. Neo-liberalism has succeeded in cementing the fortunes of the financial elites at the expense of industry and the majority of the world's population. In doing so it has made capitalism itself vulnerable to systemic collapse. The 2007–08 crisis of liquidity became a full-blown global crisis of overaccumulation on the scale not seen since the Great Depression. But, as Walden Bello (2010) emphasises, overproduction, not financial deregulation, was in fact the root cause of the current crisis.

Robert Wade (2008) notes three 'game-changing' events in the September 2008 crash that, in his words, drove an ideological stake through the efficient market hypothesis. The first of these was the collapse of three of the five major US investment banks including the bankruptcy of Lehman Brothers. The second was the US Treasury's bail out of the insurance group American International Group, Inc. (AIG). The third was the massive commitment of the US Treasury to buy up $700 billion of the toxic assets held by major banking institutions, a figure subsequently increased. The need for states to intervene on such a scale exposed the flaws in the global financial architecture. The financial services regulator had failed to ensure banks held adequate funds to protect individual bank deposits. The US and UK governments had responded to the crisis by lowering interest rates to unprecedented levels, introducing quantitative easing (pumping money into the economy) and providing huge loans to the banking sector without demanding major structural reform. By pumping money into financial institutions, Jan Kregel (2009) notes, governments have created further distortions in the economy while heavily indebting themselves, not without irony, to the financial institutions they protected. This has enabled banks to continue with their traditional trading activities without increasing lending to the real economy and bringing entire nations to the brink of bankruptcy. Without a stimulus for consumer spending the crisis is far from over. We are potentially in a situation today that Giovanni Arrighi had earlier warned of:

> Historically, the crises of overaccumulation that marked the transition from one organizational structure to another also created the conditions for the emergence of ever more powerful governmental and business agencies capable of solving the crises through a reconstitution of the capitalist world-economy on larger and more comprehensive foundations ... this process is necessarily limited in time. Sooner or later, it must reach a stage at which the crisis of overaccumulation cannot bring into existence an agency powerful enough to reconstitute the system on larger and more comprehensive foundations. (1994:330)

The ideology of neo-liberalism was one of the initial victims of the crisis, as Alessandri and Haldane's 2009 report commissioned by the Bank of England seems to indicate:

> Over the course of the past 800 years, the terms of trade between the state and banks have first swung decisively one way and then the other. For the majority of this period, the state was reliant on the deep pockets of the banks to finance periodic fiscal crises. But for at least the past century the pendulum has swung back, with the state often needing to dig deep to keep crisis-prone banks afloat.
>
> Events of the past two years have tested even the deep pockets of many states. In so doing, they have added momentum to the century-long pendulum swing. Reversing direction will not be easy. It is likely to require a financial sector reform effort every bit as radical as followed the Great Depression. It is an open question whether reform efforts to date, while slowing the swing, can bring about that change of direction.

We should not underestimate the effect of September 2008 on the collective psyche nor the challenge this poses to the already threadbare claims in support of neo-liberalism. The role of economics departments of major universities in propagating neo-liberal ideology is well documented. But attention should also be paid to the myths propagated more generally about the nature of capitalism today. This is the subject matter of the next section.

The Postmodern Spirit

The 'autonomous sphere of culture', Fredric Jameson (1993:48) writes, has expanded prodigiously to the point where everything can be said to have 'become "cultural" in some original and yet untheorised sense.' In postmodernism, *or*, the cultural logic of late capitalism, indeterminacy, playfulness, pastiche and irony are components of an ideology in which commodities are now celebrated rather than criticised. Postmodernism, in David Harvey's words, '[S]wims, even wallows, in the fragmentary and the chaotic currents of change as if that is all there is.' (2007:44) The ideology disavows materialism while embracing cultural relativism perfectly complementing the neo-liberal project and its stated aims of turning everyone into self-seeking enterprising individuals.

People appear to one another as abstract quantities while the things into which labour is embodied acquire a subjective quality. This is what Marx (1988) referred to as commodity fetishism. In this theory the measure of a thing's worth is the price it exchanges for rather than its social usefulness. And as Simon Clarke (1991) explains, commodity fetishism is not simply about the relations hidden beneath the commodity, but the processes through which commodities acquire their social power. For Clarke, the starting point of Marx's analysis is alienated labour which *precedes* capitalist property relations. This point is crucial for distinguishing the political economy of Ricardo which held that property relations are the natural base of society and Marx's *critique* of political economy which examines property as an outcome of a particular form of social relations. For Marx understood the nature of society and our relation to it as the outcome of dynamically and historically unfolding social processes and conflicts of interest. Capitalism is not a fixed entity by his reckoning; it adapts under pressure from other capitals to maintain surplus-value, doing so by developing the productive forces (machinery, infrastructures, labour in the service of production and so on) and responding to various social pressures and demands from competing class fractions. The social relations of production acquire a fetishistic form of appearance and, as Clarke has emphasised, this is not simply illusionary:

> It really is the case that the relations between individuals and things are determinate, while the relations between particular people are accidental. It really is the case that the social fate of the individual is determined by the fate of the commodities she possesses. Thus it really is the case that social relations are mediated by relations between things. (1991:103)

Markets in a certain fashion are disembedded from society the more that commodities shape our existence. Reading like a passage from Marx and Engels' *The Communist Manifesto*, Tony Blair's swansong to the Labour Party conference in 2005 rearticulated the centrality of free-market ideology to the New Labour project:

> The character of this changing world is indifferent to tradition. Unforgiving of frailty. No respecter of past reputations. It has no custom and practice … It is replete with opportunities, but they only go to those swift to adapt, slow to complain, open, willing and able to change. Unless we 'own' the future, unless our values are matched by a completely honest understanding of the reality now upon us and the next about to hit us, we will fail. And then the values we believe in become idle sentiments ripe for disillusion and disappointment. (BBC News 2005a)

Commodities do indeed batter down customs and traditions. But whereas Marx saw this as a dialectical process, for Blair the market, in Anthony Giddens' (2003) words, is a juggernaut without a driver, already naturalised and pregnant with opportunities for those who capitulate to its logic. For Reagan and Thatcher there was no need for a superego authority, no society or 'nanny' state. In Third Way, the state becomes another victim of the market; the onus is then on all of us to adjust to the problem rather than transforming the architecture.

What links Marx, Blair and many commentators concerned about globalisation is the idea that what had hitherto been thought of as solid about society is now melting in the heat of competition between capitals, a process extending far beyond national boundaries. While Marx was able to recognise this as a dialectical and by no means one-way process characterised by struggles between different class interests, Blair adopted the essentialist view of the market and property relations. Prominent theorists in contemporary sociology have questioned such perspectives while accepting a now commonsense view that all that was solid has indeed melted into air.

Beck, for example, claimed that the mentality of national self-determination would undermine the prospect of containing corporate power. 'The state's nation-based conditioning and parochialism has become an *obstacle* to inventing and developing forms of politics and statehood at the transnational level in the age of economic globalisation', he said (Beck 2006:87). Therefore, a 'cosmopolitan' democracy was needed to guarantee local autonomy in the face of the free-market juggernaut. This 'destandardised, fragmented, plural "underemployment system" was characterised by highly flexible, time-intensive and spatially decentralised forms of deregulated paid labour' (Beck 2000:70). In such a hazardous environment there was little way of telling what the future would hold, yet people would have to make strategic and thus risky decisions concerning the future. In this risk society, class had become a 'zombie category' that sociologists in denial of changes towards individualism had clung onto. Class could no longer explain social differences because as a category it was bound to a traditional conception of household and nation. People's orientations, Beck said, exceed such boundaries; their mobility signals a cosmopolitan perspective of individualistic cultures and lifestyles, a disembedding without re-embedding. Thus we should recognise that inequality had increased because of non-class processes of 'individualisation' (Beck & Beck-Gernsheim 2002).

Zygmunt Bauman (2006) has made a number of important observations about subjectivity and society today, some of which are elaborated on in later chapters. However, we find within his work postmodern tropes of disembeddedness, mobility and fluidity. His 'liquid modernity' thesis describes melting and flowing boundaries, identities and traditions. For Bauman, a liquid modernity contrasts with the more 'totalitarian' uniformity of a Fordist 'heavy/solid/condensed/systemic modernity'. In his

2008 book on consumer ethics, Bauman claims there are no more 'groups' in our 'liquid-modern' 'consumer' society, rather 'swarms' that 'assemble, disperse, and come together again from one occasion to another, each time guided by different, invariably shifting relevancies, and attracted by changing and moving targets' (2008:15). Jean Baudrillard makes a comparable point which, equally, appears to have no substance,

> We have thus become virtual monads, free electrons, individuals left to ourselves, desperately seeking the other. But the particle has no other. The other particle is always the same ... Reduced to nuclear identity, we no longer have any alternative destiny except a collision with our antagonistic double. (2001:48)

The contingent, as in non-predictable, complex, multiple and friction-free movements of objects, has become a focal point of leading figures in sociology. Similarly to Beck, John Urry claims that because we are no longer oriented to a territorial logic of nation or class even the notion 'society' is therefore of limited sociological value. We should focus, he says, on the 'complex assemblages between different mobilities that may make and contingently maintain social connections across varied social distances' (Urry 2007:48). But the premise for such arguments is false. People, by and large, remain in the locality where they are born and trade and financial flows are heavily concentrated in the dominant economies where the majority of leading companies still remain.[4] As the Argentinean sociologist Atilio Boron puts it (1999:62), '[H]uman societies have demonstrated a series of regularities in both their structures and their historical course of evolution, putting them much closer to a state of equilibrium – not in the Parsonian sense of the term, nor in its neoclassical version – than to the extreme of chaos.'

While contributing valuable insights on social processes and relations, Beck, Bauman and Urry have misinterpreted the character and overplayed the significance of post-industrialism, the virtual economy and free markets. This has implications for how we think about and respond to problems inherent to capitalism. If we believe that capitalism has changed fundamentally then we cannot rely on Marx as our source for explaining why we are currently living through another economic crisis or how it is that global resources have been exploited to the extent that the ecosystem has become such a threat to the human species (see Chapter 6). Without Marx we cannot appreciate how we have got here, why things appear the way they do and what needs to be done to prevent the sort of social, political, economic and ecological catastrophes that appear on our horizon (see below).

Michael Hardt and Antonio Negri have also rejected Marx's labour theory of value and in doing so have exposed the limitations in their own interpretation of Marx. What makes them more interesting from a Marxist perspective than the aforementioned theorists is that in accepting that capitalism has fundamentally changed they then proceed to identify weaknesses in the system that people can exploit for revolutionary purposes. Their ideas help to illustrate the problems that critical theory has created for itself by adopting a script approved by hegemonic powers. As Panitch and Konings write,

> to analyse the financial dynamics of the past decades within the terms of that era's hegemonic self-representation – that is, through the key tenets of neoliberal ideology: the retreat of public institutions from social and economic life, and the return to a pre-Keynesian era of non-intervention. But it was only on the most stylized and superficial reading that the state could be seen to have withdrawn. (2009:1)

Immaterial Capitalism

Plumbers, policemen, politicians and poets are service workers. But the taps they mend, the truncheons they swing, the tables they place their dossiers on and the trophies they collect from sponsored award shows are produced in factories by the raw power and knowledge of workers. The products, whether computers or the information put on them, are produced and consumed over time. But we could be forgiven today for believing that all labour is now 'immaterial' and that such labour can no longer be thought of as exploited labour in Marx's sense of the word.

Immaterial labour tends to refer to the kind of work done outside of the workplace often involving computer technologies but generally referring to any form of activity used by capital though not able to be quantified by direct measurements of input/time. Immaterial labour has been described as an affective or emotional form of labour producing and circulating states of being, feelings and wellbeing: desire, ease and passion. It has sister terms such as 'knowledge economy' and 'new' capitalism which Kevin Doogan (2009, 44) describes as 'a confluence of narratives that captures and represents the world in terms of abstract, self-sustaining social processes.' Hardt and Negri's *Empire*, described as the *Communist Manifesto* for the twenty-first century, maps the operational strengths and weaknesses of this new form of capitalism. Their ideas are an object example of why new capitalism needs to be recast.[5]

Hardt and Negri (2001:347) describe communication as 'the form of capitalist production in which capital has succeeded in submitting society entirely and globally to its regime, suppressing all alternative paths.' With power so dispersed, states are no longer capable of managing capitalism in a territorial way. The state is replaced with a global network of power or *Empire* armed and defended by the US military, its wealth or money circulated by institutions such as the IMF, World Bank, WTO and the Group of Eight (G8; France, Germany, Italy, Japan, the UK and the US), and the Internet functioning as the site of communication or democracy.

Empire is a diffuse, anonymous network of globalising power that is both everywhere and nowhere; it is spread so thin as to be vulnerable at all points around the globe to rebellion. Power is akin to the thin topsoil that sustains the incredible growth of a rainforest always in danger of being stripped of its nutrients at the slightest exposure to the sun. It is a world in which power is without bound or limits, a 'spatial totality' that effectively 'suspends history and thereby fixes the existing state of affairs for eternity' and penetrates at the deepest possible level (Hardt & Negri 2001:xiv).

Uprooted from the place of the factory, the now factory-less post-Fordist worker lacks a constituent identity and becomes what Hardt and Negri (2005:99) call the multitude, singularities '[W]hose difference cannot be reduced to sameness, a difference that remains different ...' In this form of production surplus-value is increasingly derived from intangible 'intellectual, immaterial and communicative' labour power which the worker rents to the capitalist who in turn provides the technologies it can use to its own advantage, freeing the worker from the monitoring and control of a capital now reduced to a parasitic function feeding on this newly socialised labour. Capitalism, in this respect, is an external force not an internal relation as Marx conceived of it. Under these circumstances the multitude engage in 'biopolitical' struggles rather than class struggles, a term Hardt and Negri take from Foucault and refashion (see Hardt & Negri 2009:56) to mean the production of subjectivities that have the potential to challenge disciplinary forms of administrative power favoured by government and employers.

Hardt and Negri's argument can be broken down into four interrelated points. First, power is dispersed through anonymous deterritorialised networks. Second, production occurs 'off-site' and beyond the clock. Third, as a consequence, labour is increasingly self-determining. Fourth, power is vulnerable at every point to biopolitical rebellion.

Point one underestimates the role of specific states and territorially entrenched corporations in creating, preserving and benefiting from the architecture of global trade, finance and informational networks of immaterial distribution. With regard to informational capital, van Ark, et al. (2003) examined the amount of GDP that industries using information and communication technologies (ICT) contribute to the US and EU economies. In the year 2000, ICT-using industries contributed 30.6 per cent of GDP to the US economy whereas industries not using ICT contributed 62 per cent of GDP. In the same year the figure for the EU was 27 per cent, leaving non-ICT-using industries to make up 67 per cent of GDP (van Ark, et al. 2003:89). The crash of the dot.com industries is a sober reminder of the limits of the knowledge economy. And as Doogan (2009:50) shows, material communication is still important when we consider that global paper consumption has increased from 131 million metric tonnes in 1975 to 352 million metric tonnes in 2005.

Point two, that production occurs offsite, also exaggerates the dominance of informational capital, delinking it from manufacture and the time and use of resources in producing and processing information. Without labour, tools such as computers would have no productive value. A capitalist who purchases machines also has to employ labour to operate them. Marx called the combination of labour and machinery the organic composition of capital; competition forces capital into purchasing more machinery while also reducing labour costs. As labour is the only force of production (a machine-like force when it actively generates value) with the capacity to exceed its reproductive value, the greater the ratio of machines to labour the more the capacity to increase surplus-value through increases in the absolute (time) and relative (efficiency) exploitation of labour diminishes. However, the worth of labour to the productive process is only realised at the point of exchange. A capitalist cannot determine in advance of exchange whether the labour he employs will generate values in excess of its reproductive value and therefore cannot calculate through a simple measurement of labour time the value of the commodity. As Starosta explains, the general social relations between private and independent producers regulate the price of commodities, such as when supermarkets reduce prices to compete with one another. A big budget movie, for example, involves hundreds of 'knowledge workers' (2008:309); but if the film is a box office flop, the value of that labour is worthless; the initial investment enters into circulation and profit is generated when the film is successful.

The situation is complex as Marx had understood when he wrote that 'Now that we know the *substance* of value. It is *labour*. We know the *measure of its magnitude*. It is *labour-time*. The *form*, which stamps *value as exchange-value*, remains to be analysed' (emphasis in original, 1988:131). This at least tells us one thing: that the value of the commodity, according to Marx, cannot be determined as an aggregate of physiological labour. However, this is precisely how Hardt and Negri present the labour theory of value. By interpreting this as an embodied theory of value in which profit is measured by the average amount of abstract labour time it takes to make a product Hardt and Negri (2005:114–15) are then able to claim that the theory no longer holds. Immaterial labour would indeed pose a problem if we conceive of labour in the standard image of the embodied worker clocking into the factory in the morning and clocking out in the afternoon when sufficient value has been contributed to the process.

Regarding point three, accepting for the moment that their interpretation of value is correct and that much production now occurs outside of the factory, there is no logical reason why, even in these circumstances, labour would exceed the control of capital. If anything, the opposite is happening. Information systems are being used to introduce new ways of quantifying and controlling immaterial labour, such as in the university sector where academic work is measured by student evaluations of teaching, quantity of publications, the ranking of journals they appear in, the number of citations registered on Google Scholar, external grant applications, participation in influential networks and so on. Deleuze (1992) claimed that we are moving away from disciplinary enclosures such as the school, hospital and family towards societies of control in which people are reduced to measureable units, codes, samples, data markets or *dividuals* (more on this in later chapters). This is undertheorised in Hardt and Negri's work.

Point four concerns the power of the multitude. According to the argument of Hardt and Negri (2005:217), 'Each struggle remains singular and tied to its local conditions but at the same time is immersed in the common web'. Lula's Workers Party (Partido dos Trabalhadores; PT) in Brazil recognises and nurtures this potential, they say, by engaging in direct dialogue with the movements, gaining autonomy from international capital by paying off the IMF and encouraging forms of biopolitical struggle by prioritising an equilibrium of power in struggles against social inequalities. In this version of struggle, there is no clear sense of the different, often contradictory, values, strategies and effectiveness of each movement. They are all in some vague fashion engaged in biopolitical struggle. Accordingly, we could claim that a lorry driver protest against fuel prices is one-of-a-kind with workers striking in Greece in protest at the state's capitulation to the IMF. Are we to believe then that struggles against austerity measures of European governments are biopolitical? Their argument is obscure.

Žižek's and Hardt and Negri's positions differ in that the former regards the state as the condition that makes the multitude possible by regulating a space for people to engage in immaterial production. To confront this power, the multitude would have to negate itself by forming a movement closer to the Leninist model of a mass party and therefore express itself as a class. Yet Žižek also appears to endorse Hardt and Negri's reading of immaterial labour such as when he claims that the 'rise of "intellectual" labour ... to a hegemonic position ... undermines the standard notion of exploitation, since it is no longer labour-time which serves as the source and ultimate measure of value' (2010:240). Another example of why, according to Žižek, this theory no longer holds is that Venezuela as a socialist republic exploits poorer countries through the sale of its oil. However, Marx is very clear on this point: exploitation relates to the use capital makes of labour power for the purposes of surplus-value. A nation state cannot exploit other nation states in this sense.

Žižek is clearly a serious scholar of Marx who self-identifies as a Marxist. However, like Hardt and Negri, and others above, he appears to accept that capitalism has fundamentally changed and that Marx's labour theory of value no longer holds. It is not 'new' capitalism that undermines the labour theory of value; capitalism in whatever form does not fit the description attributed to Marx by Hardt and Negri, and Žižek. Marx had already recognised in the nineteenth century the flaws in the embodied theory of value, particularly in Ricardo's work. As Simon Clarke explains, Ricardo's theory 'identified labour *immediately* with its social forms, as value, wages, rent and profit.' (1991:98) Marx, on the other hand, derives the categories of political economy 'from capitalism as a form of social production whose social character is only expressed in the alienated form of the exchange of commodities under the rule of money' (Clarke 1991:74). The basis of Žižek's rejection of the labour theory of value, most explicit in his critique of Cohen, is flawed. Žižek writes,

> Gerald A. Cohen has enumerated the four features of the classical Marxist notion of the working class: (1) it constitutes the majority of society; (2) it produces the wealth of society; (3) it consists of the exploited members of society; (4) its members are the needy people in society. When these four features are combined, they generate two further features: (5) the working class has nothing to lose from revolution; (6) it can and will engage in a revolutionary transformation of society. (2008a:420)

However, the working class is made up of a number of ideological factions each with varying stakes in the economy, whereas points five and six are non-sequiturs. Žižek then writes that, 'None of the first four features applies to the contemporary working class, which is why features (5) and (6) cannot be generated.' (2008a:420) For all his criticisms of capitalism, its apparatuses of power and left-liberal ideology, Žižek appears wedded to a script that people he is critical of has written. Simon Clarke is worth quoting again when he says that,

> [W]hatever may be the basis of the subjective identification of capitalists and workers, this does not in any way undermine the fundamental objective character of their opposing class interests and the objective determination of their life experience and prospects by their class position. (Cited in Saad-Filho & Johnston 2005:54)

Ontologies and epistemologies of different theorists are not always so easy to map onto one another, and Žižek's analysis sometimes suffers from this problem; however, by making decisions about how we stretch concepts, more or less, into an operational fit, we gain useful insights into the complex relations between people in society. Žižek's work is exemplary of this and has been vital in reviving interest in Marx among a left that had rightly opposed more dogmatic versions of Marxism, but in doing so had veered towards postmodern relativism. We do not need to create a straw man in Marx in order to develop Marx's theory through psychoanalytic and socio-linguistic approaches to ideology. We do not have to claim we live in a 'liquid modernity' to show that relationships between one another are today more fragile and our futures more uncertain than before the last major crisis of overaccumulation in the 1970s. It does not follow that because the working class is no longer the political force it once was that the days of class struggle are well and truly over. History shows us time and again that the social dynamics and processes Marx identified are alive and well in capitalism today. By remaining with Marx we can also anticipate how current crises are likely to unfold.

End-Capitalism

Terry Eagleton writes, 'It is just that one can no longer doubt, watching the remorseless *centralising* of the contingent, the dogmatic privileging of what escapes over what does not, the constant dissolution of dialectics, that one is in the presence of a full-blooded ideology.' (1992:138) The risks of economic collapse and environmental devastation are real and present. We are now in a phase that it is appropriate to call *end-capitalism*, a materially and ideologically exposed capitalism forever on the brink of collapse. However, with knowledge of the material problems of capitalism but without the ideological anchoring points to critique it in its totality, we beget what Peter Sloterdijk (2008) calls enlightened false-consciousness: a knowledge of the problems we face but cynicism as to the possibility of doing anything about it. So what is at stake?

Crises do often manifest themselves as contingent moments: 9/11, the collapse of Lehman Brothers, the Deepwater Oilrig disaster and soon, perhaps, the much-anticipated 'tipping point' that leads to the rapid collapse of the ecosystem. But while the specifics of the event cannot be predicted, we can anticipate that something along such lines could realistically happen. We can differentiate, more or less, between hysterical and obscurantist apocalyptic visions, and warnings of economic and ecological catastrophe based on empirical evidence. The financial crash was predictable. Future crises, tipping points and apocalypses are already written into the script of capitalism. Whether because of fiscal tightening by European governments, the failure to properly regulate finance or the longer-term decline in profitability, it seems likely that the economic crisis will continue and probably worsen.

Referring to the 'four horsemen of the apocalypse', Žižek (2010) identifies four major threats to humankind. The first, and probably most significant of these, is ecological catastrophe (see Chapter 6), precipitated after a 'tipping point' when there is a qualitative, catastrophic, irreparable and chaotic change in the ecosystem. The second is 'intellectual property rights', which create a legal basis for a potential commodification of everything including our genes. The third is techno-scientific advancements such as genetic engineering and nano-technology; advancements in these areas allow for the control and manipulation of human life down to the level of microorganisms. The exclusion of millions of the earth's habitants either behind heavily policed walls or contained in ever expanding urban slums is the fourth of the horsemen.

The metaphorically excessive and causal 'fifth' horseman is the one that we can claim with some degree of certainty will lead to a tipping point of one kind or another. The economy is the background for all the four horsemen; the likelihood of any of these predictions being realised depends on what happens to the economy. There are correlations between economic crises and global warming, the growth of urban slums, the misappropriation of new technologies and the commodification of the commons. The global financial crisis is the clearest sign yet that an apocalypse of a kind is on the horizon. István Mészáros (2010) describes the seriousness of the crisis when he writes that it is 'not the greatest crisis in human history but the greatest crisis in all senses. Economic crises cannot be separated from the rest of the system.'

To remain profitable, capital must constantly expand; but as it does so, it runs the risk of oversupplying the market with products for which there is no longer a demand. This is the situation we are in today. 'The real barrier of capitalist production', Marx said, 'is capital itself' (quoted in Bello 2010:277). So the question is, how does capital counteract this tendency? Neo-liberalism was one such response, financialisation another and a third was 'the integration of semi-capitalist, pre-capitalist, and non-capitalist areas into the capitalist system' (Bello 2010:277). This relates to what Harvey (2005b) and others have called a spatio-temporal fix. China, for a time, was seen as such a fix when it embarked on a programme of rapid industrialisation by opening its markets to foreign investment. China was able to capitalise on its vast human resources, cheap labour or potential future consumers. This was something of a double-edged sword for the west though. Walden Bello (2010) points out that while for the past two decades the Chinese economy has grown between roughly 8 per cent and 10 per cent and has been the principal source of capitalist growth, there is still insufficient internal demand for its industrial product. As a consequence, Chinese industry has oversupplied the market with goods that even western consumers can no longer afford to purchase, thereby exacerbating the problem of overaccumulation in the west. With 1.3 billion people on average yearly earnings of just $285 there, the Chinese economy is unlikely to be able to absorb this surplus anytime soon (Bello 2010:280).[6]

So, if economies such as China, now the second largest in the world, are unlikely to compensate for falling rates of profit in the west, where is demand going to come from? We are currently, at the time of writing, seeing governments across Europe embark on savage cuts to public sector funding. This is likely to increase unemployment, drive demand down further, and precipitate civil unrest and authoritarian responses. After a week of coordinated strikes across Europe in late September 2010, Michael Hudson writing in the US online newsletter *Counterpunch* argues that 'the Neoliberal Revolution seeks to achieve in Europe what the United States has achieved since real wages stopped rising in 1979: doubling the share of wealth enjoyed by the richest 1 per cent. This involves reducing the middle class to poverty, breaking union power, and destroying the internal market as a precondition.'

We are entering the next stage of a class war and for it to be visible we need to break the post-political consensus. Much is at stake. As Žižek writes,

> In today's post-political democracy, the traditional bipolarity between a Social-Democratic Centre-Left and a Conservative Centre-Right is gradually being replaced by a new bipolarity between politics and post-politic: the technocratic-liberal multiculturalist-tolerant part of post-political administration and its Rightist-popular counterpart of passionate political struggle. (2010:ix)

There are portents of the sort of authoritarianism that Žižek and others have warned of in the Tea Party, Berlusconi and China (as an authoritarian model for capitalist development). China is far from being the ideal-type economy for the west to mimic, but its form of authoritarian governance is more likely to appeal. There would still be the need to arrest and reverse a long-term decline in profitability though and interventionist strategies are also prone to failure. As Mészáros explains:

> The larger the dose administered to the convalescing patient, the greater is the dependency on the wonder drug. That is, the graver the symptoms of capitalist cost accounting. These symptoms menacingly foreshadow the ultimate paralysis and breakdown of capitalist production and expansion... what is supposed to be the remedy turns out to be a contributory cause of further crisis... (2010:83)

The massive state-bailouts of the finance sector are likely to produce the same effect. Surplus has to go somewhere though, and if China is not the answer there are no other obvious candidates for capitalist expansion because, as David Harvey puts it, much of the world has already been integrated into the capitalist system: 'At some point quantitative changes lead to qualitative shifts and we need to take seriously the idea that we may be at exactly such an inflexion point in the history of capitalism.' (2010:217)

The constant circulation of spectacles of devastation and suffering raise the material realities of capitalism to the surface of ideology, thus supplanting postmodern ideology with its emphasis on issues of cultural representation (see Chapter 4). End-capitalism denotes a period in which there are no obvious ideologically palatable 'exit strategies' for hegemonic powers to embark on; in which global warming poses a real, permanent and also uneven threat to peoples and societies; in which populations are increasingly impoverished through un/der/employment while also being segregated and brutalised; in which liberal-parliamentary states veer towards more authoritarian forms of social control. These are societies in which people appear cynical, emotionally stunted and empty (see Chapter 5). The more drastic the responses of states and corporations to the events and long-term structural issues triggering or manifesting from crises, the more exposed are the flaws and injustices of the system, the more vulnerable capital is to contingent outbursts of popular anger that increasingly assume a larger strategic class character. In the dialectic of end-capitalism, the hyphen is intermittently withdrawn to invoke the imperative *end capitalism!*[7]

Conclusion

> We must be able to go on saying 'people', 'workers', 'abolition of private property', and so on, without being considered has-beens, and without considering ourselves as has-beens. (Badiou 2010:64)

Friedrich Engels described the bourgeois as 'mighty benefactors of humanity' who, through acts of charity, 'give back to the plundered victims the hundredth part of what belongs to them!' (Engels 2009:283). In more affluent times the consumer also stages acts of charity when purchasing Fairtrade alternatives. But the capacity to consume such products is now brought into question by the current crisis. The once-affluent middle classes and aspirant working class are prone to harden their position against whatever person or abstract entity can be held to blame for whatever predicament we find ourselves in. As different views on the causes of the crisis circulate, it is now more than ever that we need what Alain Badiou calls the communist hypothesis.

Badiou writes that,

> For three decades now, the word "communism" has been either totally forgotten or practically equated with criminal enterprises. That is why the subjective situation of politics has everywhere become so incoherent. Lacking the Idea, the popular masses's confusion is inescapable. (2010:258)

So what is communism? It is, says Badiou,

> [A]n egalitarian society which, acting under its own impetus, brings down walls and barriers; a polyvalent society, with variable trajectories, both at work and in our lives. But 'communism' also means forms of political organisation that are not modelled on spatial hierarchies. (2010:61)

This also means clarifying what Marx understood by alienation, exploitation and surplus-value while also distinguishing what has changed since Marx's day from what remains essentially the same. There are material grounds for thinking that the game is not over and that Žižek's call for the 'politics of the impossible' is not mere wishful thinking. But if labour is now immaterial then politics proper, which organised labour is pivotal to, would indeed be impossible and Hardt and Negri's propositions would have to be taken more seriously. Thankfully, capitalism has not changed as much as some have supposed.

Sean Sayers writes, with reference to Marx, that, 'All ideas are social and historical products. All ideas are, in this sense, ideological. Critical ideas – just like uncritical ones – arise from and reflect social reality.' (2007:108) We have for a long while been in the midst of a kind of deconstructive pseudo-activity[8] of micro struggles that respond to the symptoms of capitalism though without ever challenging the totality. We have fixated on symptoms – HIV/AIDS in Africa, consumer waste and so on – for which simple solutions are available – charity, recycling and so on – without disturbing business or addressing the inherent problem. As Žižek contends, ideology is rendered both meaningless (there are no ideological antagonisms except within the coordinates of the system's self representation which includes fundamentalism as a symbolic adversary) but also omnipresent (ideology is at its most effective when it is invisible to us). This is hopefully starting to change.

The following chapters identify, explain and elaborate the different ways we tie ourselves in ideological knots with this most destructive mode of production. These knots are identifiable in general subjective formations inhering in the socio-historical context that confirms what Marx and Engels (1989) had said about human subjectivity, that 'The phantoms formed in the human brain are also, necessarily, sublimates of their material life-process, which is empirically verifiable and bound to material premises.' In this socio-historic moment, to put it in Badiou's words, 'we have to be bold enough to have an idea. A great idea.' (2010:66)

3

NAKED ENTERPRISE

Man is dominated by the making of money, by acquisition as the ultimate purpose of his life. Economic acquisition is no longer subordinated to man as the means for the satisfaction of his material needs. This reversal of what we should call the natural relationship, so irrational from a naive point of view, is evidently as definitely a leading principle of capitalism as it is foreign to all peoples not under capitalistic influence. At the same time it expresses a type of feeling which is closely connected with certain religious ideas. Thus, if we ask why should 'money be made out of men', Benjamin Franklin himself, although he was a colourless deist, answers in his autobiography with a quotation from the Bible which his strict Calvinistic father had drummed into him again and again in his youth: 'Seest thou a man diligent in his business? He shall stand before kings' (Weber 2003:53).

The 1982 publication *The Official Guide to Success* offers an insight into what a means/end rationality infused into an ethic of enterprise, as promulgated in neo-liberal ideology, amounts to. It advises those looking to get ahead not to 'chop the other guy's liver any finer than you have to. The future is an enigma. None of us can be certain that we'll never need something from a former boss, competitor, co-worker' (Hopkins 1985:20). Thatcher helped turn enterprise into a virtue in and of itself by promoting an 'enterprise culture' while at the same time dismantling many of the regulations that had inhibited the flexible working practices which are now a familiar feature of the labour market. Paul du Gay captures the essence of the enterprising ethic, which is, he explains,

[T]he 'kind of action or project' that exhibits 'enterprising' qualities or characteristics on the part of individuals or groups. In this latter sense an enterprise culture is one in which certain enterprising qualities – such as self-reliance, personal responsibility, boldness and a willingness to take risks in the pursuit of goals – are regarded as personal virtues and promoted as such. (1996:56)

In such lives, Colin Gordon writes, 'there is at least a sense in which one remains always continuously employed in (at least) that one enterprise, and that it is part of the continuous business of living to make adequate provision for the preservation, reproduction and reconstruction of one's own human capital' (cited in Rose 1998:161). According to this neo-Foucauldian reading, the discourse of enterprise has penetrated so deeply into the 'soul' that it has become a pre-discursive fact of life.[1]

In psychoanalytic theory the subject is in a state of permanent mental insecurity. Thatcher provided a material justification for that insecurity in creating the moral and legal framework for inducing people to be enterprising. This chapter applies some of Lacan's concepts to the topic of subjective enterprise. Whereas a business enterprise operates according to the logic of surplus-value, the worker operates according to the logic of employability, developing ways to improve job prospects through training, by gaining experiences illustrative of certain values, the cultivation and conscious projection of a kind of a personality and so on, to gain competitive advantage over other workers in the labour market. Employability is the object of enterprise, a calling of a kind.

Enterprise

Will to enterprise

The development of new productive forces leads to a demand for a new kind of worker. To meet that demand, workers have to modify themselves by developing new skills and, increasingly, refining their social personalities. As power shifts in favour of capital, workers compete with one another to be the object of the boss's desire by entering into new productive relationships in and outside of work that promise enhancements to intellectual, physical and 'social' capital. In their enterprise, workers exploit the means for enhancing their job prospects at the expense of other workers and in doing so embrace their servitude by necessity. One is compelled to be enterprising by virtue of the fact that organised labour is so weak and the demands of capital so excessive. Workers are not simply adapting to changes in the productive forces, they are adapting to the surplus demands of employers. In other words, the qualities workers are now encouraged to possess exceed the material necessities of capital and only serve to strengthen the grip of employers, both materially and ideologically, over every aspect of our lives.

Anthony Giddens said, of the changing social landscapes of post-Thatcherite Britain, that social bonds 'have effectively to be *made*, rather than inherited from the past', a 'fraught and difficult enterprise, but one also that holds out the promise of great rewards' (1994:106). If the worker has become 'disembedded' from traditional social moorings, a point that is highly contestable, her reinvention as an enterprising soul is anything but liberating. Extending Marx's analysis on the link between changes in productive forces and the social character of workers, Foucault coined the term governmentality to offer a richer description of the procedures and practices through which individuals adapt to the labour market. Individuals, he said, increasingly make use of regulatory 'technologies', reminiscent of those employed by governments to manage institutions, as a means for acquiring a normalised social character. It is through knowledge of ourselves, Foucault argued, that we are able to adapt to social change and renounce those parts of the self that fall out of line with social norms. A technology of the self is the means by which we acquire knowledge of how to conduct ourselves and develop a way of being that fits certain ideas of happiness, a balanced lifestyle, a perfect body and mind, virtue and so on. When applying for jobs we scrutinise the job descriptor, reflect on whether we possess the desired qualities and scan for more information to help craft an application that meets the demand. It does not start and end with the particular application; we have already anticipated through our education and in our own reflections the kind of job we want and the sort of qualities we need to acquire.[2]

Several years ago, I studied a document called a *Record of Achievement* that schoolchildren in England complete towards the end of their secondary level education. It fits Foucault's description of a technology of the self. The records of achievement were divided into a number of categories, some completed by the student and others by the teacher. Teachers were given instructions on what should be included. The introduction should include information on the student's punctuality, conduct and appearance. The next section concerned 'attitude to work', how effective the student is in completing tasks, working on her own and with others; the student's own reflections are included here. In the next few sections we get a sense of how far this technology extends into everyday life. First, we have the section on particular interests in and out of school. It invites the student to think about the value of 'extra-curricular' activities to employers. Second, the student writes on the work experience they had at the school's behest. The section that penetrates deepest into the personal life of individuals is the one on 'social life'. Here the student should reflect on how they get on with others, whether they are happier with a few friends or relate well to everyone, how they spend their 'free time', what 'exactly' their social life consists of, whether they see themselves as 'very lively, outgoing ... or basically shy' and whether they have 'a quiet sense of humour or ... prefer to take centre stage.'[3] This dramaturgical metaphor compares with Erving Goffman's (1971) critique of the performative practices we all engage in.

The record of achievement illustrates the extent to which the subject's lifeworld is now mapped to the employment context and how this process is embarked on prior to the subject's entry into the labour market. Such 'technologies' are deployed to enable the person to govern herself as an efficient object for surplus appropriation.

Employment agencies help us to make use of the intellectual and practical devices and procedures or technologies that aid in our job quests. We develop the know-how on what makes an employer tick and how to acquire the energy, initiative, calculation, self-reliance and personal responsibility they seek.[4]

Career guides can show us how to think about ourselves, to ask whether we are 'self-motivated', possess 'drive' or 'vitality',[5] or if we are 'doers', 'thinkers' or 'carers'.[6] Policing ourselves is freedom of a kind. It is the freedom of the individual isolated and impotent when confronting the leviathan of capital. It is crucial for businesses involved in their own competitive struggles that workers adapt themselves to perform new tasks. As the confidence of the bourgeois grows and that of the proletariat diminish, the former makes demands on subjective 'use' value over and above what is needed to keep the operation running. Skills and attributes specific to one occupation bleed into others to create a generic or 'transferrable' set of qualities that all employers now desire. We can see how, over the course of the twentieth century, skills typically associated with sales jobs are now the common currency of human capital.

Prior to 1914, candidates for white-collar jobs were often assessed for their 'tidy handwriting and boyish enthusiasm.'[7] With developments in production techniques and diversification of labour in the industrialised economies the demands on human subjectivity became more extensive. In the 1940s, Adorno and Horkheimer wrote that the 'most intimate reactions of human beings have been so thoroughly reified that the idea of anything specific to themselves now persists only as an utterly abstract notion' (1997:167). By the 1950s, C. Wright Mills noted in job advertisements for sales jobs the 'ability to get along with people and to work more co-operatively with them' and also the 'ability to meet and talk to people easily, and attractiveness in appearance' (1951:186). The employer buys the employee's 'social personalities' (Wright Mills 1951:182).

In the 1980s, Arlie Hochschild (2003) studied the pressures flight attendants were under to smile and express enthusiasm for the sake of the passenger's satisfaction. The worker labours her emotions and exhausts them in the process. The 'human relations' industry, said Jean Baudrillard, were the 'cultural designers' integrating the worker 'into a single formal shell, to facilitate interaction in the name of the promotion of culture, to promote an ambience for people, as design does for objects.' (1998:109) In the

1990s, Catherine Casey (1995:152) argued that corporations were trying to restore a Protestant ethic of dedication and deference by integrating into the firm a worker's social character. Contemporary management discourse, writes Paul Du Gay, presents 'work not as a painful obligation imposed on individuals, nor as an activity undertaken for mainly instrumental purposes, but rather as a vital means to individual liberty and self-fulfilment.' (2000:64) Employers across a range of industries and occupations make excessive demands on the subjectivity of the worker who, in seeing herself as an individual possessed with the capacity to determine her own future, is the ideal embodiment of what Giddens falsely identifies as an autotelic self. And, as István Mészáros puts it, 'Self-seeking egoistic fulfilment is the straitjacket imposed by capitalist development on man, and the values of "individual autonomy" represent its ethical glorification.' (2005:258)

Culture of employability

In recent texts on the labour market there is a certain presupposition that work is inherently insecure. To counter these claims, Kevin Doogan uses evidence from European, US and Canadian labour market surveys that show employment and long-term employment has increased in the period between 1991 and 2002 (2009:173). Workplace militancy, he says, is undermined because workers come to accept the employer's and, ironically, trade union claims that jobs are vulnerable to external competition. However materially secure work is, the point that Doogan is not refuting is that people *feel* insecure and their attitude towards work is likely to reflect this. Then again, regardless of how people feel, they have no choice other than to develop a social personality that employers want. By projecting the self in a certain way employment prospects are improved, whether in the firm or in the general labour market context. The private lives of individuals become signifiers of commensurability with capital. Taking this a step further, to be employable means being like the employer, being his mirror double.[8]

Whenever we look into a mirror we see another, the image of self, returning our gaze. As Lacan argued, the reflected image 'sees' us and, as we in turn imagine what it sees, we create an identity for ourselves. This identity is always predicated on what we imagine others want to see. The self is created around a need to compensate for or cover over the inconsistencies that inhibit our symbolic inclusion in the world; in other words, there is an ontological gap between language and reality that ideology fills, the lack in the other that Lacan calls the *objet a* or object cause of desire. The subject is therefore a *fantasy* construct developed through what we consciously and unconsciously suppose the other wants. Essentially, we all want to be likeable to others; we all want to be likeable to the image that reflects our gaze.

The mirror double is not simply a literal reflection of the person. It can be any object – a face in a magazine, or a particular group or authority – whose image is sympathetic to the idea we have of ourselves. Developing Lacan's argument, Althusser describes the subject as a self-constituting image of ideology brought into existence the moment she misrecognises herself in the authority that hails or interpellates her. Authorities such as the school, family, media, employer and so on are the collective embodiment of this, which Althusser called ideological state apparatuses. For both Lacan and Althusser, language plays a vital role in naming the subject. The identities we assume for ourselves are not only misrecognised as the authentic substance of our being but also constrain us by providing a frame into which to fit our behaviours to afford consistency with our own sense of who we are and, more importantly, with the symbolic order of an imagined society into which we invest power and meaning. The position I develop shares with Althusser the argument that the subject is a product of capital but differs in two important respects. First, interpellation is indirect. Capital does not want a passive subject. It wants us to 'read' clues, think through strategies for improving job prospects and reflect on the use-values of subjectivity and how they could benefit exchange. Second, there is a genuine capacity to deny interpellation in regard to employment, to turn away from the employer as the authority hailing us, by identifying with ideologies that are hostile to capitalism. The problem is that materially we have no choice, if we are to be in contention for a job, other than to respond to the authority hailing us and develop and promote the skills and characteristics employers demand. We are still interpellated in a certain way.

When an employer casts his gaze, the question we must consciously ask of ourselves is whether the gaze is the one reflected in our mirror. This was a question posed in the *Guardian*, Britain's premier broadsheet newspaper of the left. A marketing assistant wrote to the resident job-advice columnist Irene Krechowiecka that,

> I keep missing out on promotions to management positions despite the fact I have a reputation for being hard-working and reliable. What am I doing wrong?
>
> HD,
> Marketing Assistant, Leicester

[Reply:]

It's a mistake to expect promotion in return for doing your job well or being conscientious …

Being described as a hard worker can sometimes mean you're seen as struggling to keep up, poor at delegating or not enough of a team player. It's not so much hard work that gets rewarded, but working hard at whatever is seen as significant by those in charge …

Those who appear to have meteoric career progression are quick to pick up on the management's latest pet project and become involved in it. They are even faster at distancing themselves from work that's losing its prestige …

Because advancement is their main priority, they put effort into areas that are sure to win approval in a way that gets noticed. Managers promote in their own image, so study the behaviour, appearance and language of those who've leapfrogged you. How do they fit in with the organisation, and what could you do to be more like that?

If the idea of modelling yourself on the management fills you with horror, that could be the reason you're not getting the chance to join them.

Irene Krechowiecka, *rise* (2002:4)

The advice might seem excessive, a parody even; however, the tone is serious and the content consistent with much of the literature on careers. In this example, the marketing assistant does not know why her efforts are not being rewarded. She doubts the quality of her work even though, according to Krechowiecka, the failure to secure promotion has nothing to do with output. She needs to become the mirror double of her boss. This means trying to decipher what it is they want. As Lacan said, the problem, and the reason why this particular individual felt compelled to write to Krechowiecka, is that the other's desire is an enigma. The assistant has to 'read' from the 'clues' in other people's behaviour what the boss might want from her. She needs to be the one who fills in for what he lacks, the *objet a*, by possessing the attributes the employer demands, what he supposes is the use-value of her labour as relevant to the particular mode of employment. The worker assumes the symbolic position of the lack in the employer: the vacancy that needs filling.

Adorno and Horkheimer (1997) refer to a process they call pseudo-individualisation. Minor variations are manufactured into standardised products to lend them an individual quality. The pseudo-individual identifies something of herself in these variations, and the more she does so the more the product becomes a substitute for her own identity. In buying a tanning product we acquire the healthy-looking skin that we are manipulated into wanting. In a similar way to the consumer of an individualised product, the worker makes up for what is presented to her as lacking, a skill, qualification, experience or personal quality, by buying into employability and in doing so becomes a fragment of herself. The problem for the employer is that it has to compete with other employers, whether for surplus-value or for the best job candidates. The employer always strives for more. And as the employer strives for more, the worker too, in competition with other workers, also has to strive for more. The best job candidates may have an easier ride into employment and are able to make higher demands on the employer, but they also set the bar for weaker candidates. Whatever our abilities, we have to sacrifice something of our selves to become like(able to) the employer.

Enterprise has an object. That object for capital is profit. The object for the worker is employability which promises a wage and job satisfaction. In employability lurks the fantasy of the ideal job, a desire for something beyond our current experience of the labour market.

Desire gives shape, direction and a sense of purpose to our lives. The subject who desires, Lacan said, desires to desire. What we consciously desire is often achievable; the object *cause* of desire is not. So, in the case of employability the object of desire might for example be a skill or a certificate; in the context of labour the object *cause* of desire is employability, a 'thing' that we can never get enough of if we want to remain in permanent contention for work. Employability is both an object of desire – a thing we consciously recognise as desirable – and the object cause of desire – the impossible object that shapes and conditions desire, the *objet a* or lack in capital. With employability as the object cause of the worker's desire, every object of use-value (skill and so on) that we consciously desire, once possessed, fails ultimately to satisfy capital: 'it' is never satisfied, we are never employable enough.

The worker desires the object of employability as a marker of the boss's desire. In desiring continued employment, higher salaries, and more status, responsibility and security, the worker desires to desire employability, a thing we can never satisfy. A 'good value-added strategy', Harry Freedman (2009) on *The Guardian* newspaper careers blog writes, is 'built around three simple qualities: competency, enthusiasm and dependency … Merely having the ability to do the job is not enough to demonstrate value.'

The word employability therefore has no fixed meaning. It operates as an empty or Master signifier associated with combinations of minor terms.[9] The master signifier, Lacan explains, is like an upholstery button of a cushion that gathers together the fluff or 'floating' signifiers contained inside.[10,11] Employability 'quilts' or gathers together the fluff of 'enterprise', 'ethics' and 'enjoyment' into the law of surplus-value. It brings disconnected words such as 'communication', 'teamwork', 'flexibility', 'enthusiasm' and 'social responsibility' into proximity with one another to become the fluff or 'assets', 'marketing and deployment skills' and 'presentation' to reflect 'the personal and labour market context' (Tamkin & Hillage 1999). Employers can decide which of these apply to them and what then to look for in their present and future employees. The worker has to attach the tail to the donkey, to quilt the fluff at the point that nails the job and be 'proactive when faced with ill-defined circumstances', as Richard Sennett (2006:51) says.

Employability homogenises into an exchange relation the heterogeneous use–values of subjectivity, attitudes, experiences, skills, human qualities and characteristics. From a storehouse of use-values, the worker cherry-picks the ripest for exchange, wisely discarding those that have gone rotten. As the UK job website Monster (2010a) advises, 'be careful not to give valuable space to insignificant achievements. As you refine your curriculum vitae (CV), discard any content that is not selling you in the right way.'

Employability is a generic term for the 'transferrable skills' that many employers want:

> self-awareness; self-management; interpersonal skills; flexibility; communication; problem solving; team-working; business awareness; networking; negotiation; leadership; computer literacy; language skills; driving ability. (Foster 1998:12)

The UK government career website describes transferrable skills as those 'built up during any job or activity that you can apply to other jobs. You can build up skills through all sorts of activities – jobs, projects, volunteer work, hobbies, sports, virtually anything.'

Demands shift to reflect the changing needs of employers caught in the vortex of their own competitive struggles. The weakness of organised labour is reflected in the opportunity for employers to keep demanding more. In crisis times, the US JobWeb website (2010) advises that 'it's a buyer's market, meaning, employers have a minimum number of positions to fill, so they're going to be rather picky about the credentials of the new graduates they hire.' As the boss chases new ways to generate profit, the worker is forced to act like an entrepreneur, to seek out ways to profit from the resources possessed and those potentially within grasp.[12] Both need to remain ahead of their respective competitors but the power is always skewed to favour the boss. In the context of the economic downturn, the *Guardian* (Bachelor 2010) informs us on its jobs website that 'you may have to take a salary decrease to ensure you continue working.' The term workplace militancy does not figure in their lexicon.

The boss of it all

We are never employable enough. Employability operates as a kind of object cause of desire, the thing always wanted and never obtained, onto which, like a comfort blanket promising security, we accumulate the detritus of skills and attributes employers seem to want. These insure against possible unemployment and sustain hope that a better job and life is somewhere over the horizon. Employability is the worker's death drive. The ego has to think of itself in its idealised form as seen in the perceived eyes of employers, a general category (the plurality of employers) rather than a specific entity (the specific employer). The actual employer plays second fiddle to *employers*, the latter constituting market demands operating as a singular *boss of it all*. The boss of it all is the ideal employer of the future, the gatekeeper policing entry to a better life. Every stage of exploitation is a stepping-stone along the slow march to ideal employment. Another day and another imagined boss enters our lives, another set of demands, another object of desire. It is an imagined boss in the sense that we project on to the employer as an abstract entity the qualities we imagine, not without cause, the ideal-ego/worker possesses. In the field I work in, that person probably has high teaching evaluations, publications in top ranking journals, one or two books and research grants, and belongs to a number of academic networks. Regardless of the motivations for writing it, this book helps me along the way to the perfect academic post. Sooner or later, we have to think about things we do out of conviction in terms of enterprise.

Developing the qualities that only a particular employer wants is not an option for anyone who does not want to be dependent on that one employer for ongoing employment. The subject cannot do anything other than desire what employers in the abstract desire. The boss of all bosses, the boss of it all, is a spectral presence haunting our lives. His demands are both pervasive and insatiable.

This notion of the boss of it all corresponds to Lacan's definition of the 'big' or imagined Other, the symbolic eyes of society. Socialisation into the symbolic order occurs when we develop a competence in the (m)Other's tongue, a language that is initially and always to a degree foreign to us.[13] It is a language we never master, a tongue we never have self-determination over. It is as if the organ of the tongue is a foreign body possessing us, speaking on our behalf. In an ongoing process of learning from other people's words, gestures and actions we gain awareness of what certain words, gestures and actions signify. We learn to be likeable by discerning what makes the other tick, unconsciously identifying with social norms. As such, it is not one person's language we have to learn but the language of society, the big Other. And so perpetual anxiety derives from the fact that language is always to a degree foreign to us. Because language is not ours to determine, we can never be sure of how our utterances will be interpreted by others. This is why we often use devices such as a 'smiley' in a text message to help fix potentially ambiguous statements and feel anxious when friends take a long time in responding to personal emails.

We can never be sure of what the big Other wants, we can never be sure what the boss of all bosses – the big Boss – wants. The labour market is like a fantasy frame showing us how to desire. Think, for example, of the abundance of signifiers in a high street making up what we come to recognise as a place where certain activities, in this case shopping, take place. The activity of shopping in a particular street is something we do without thinking about the complex interactions shopping entails. The high street is the form showing us how to desire and thus enabling us to act out among those signs behaviours that have common meaning. The labour market shows us how to shop for employability.

The UK graduate *Prospects Directory* (2010) reminds us that the big Boss is with us in leisure time. Do not 'overlook your hobbies and interests, voluntary work or community involvement' it says: they are evidence of your abilities and it is important 'to start thinking about yourself in this way because employers will.' It haunts us in periods of unemployment. Lisa Bachelor (2009) of the *Guardian* newspaper jobs-section warns of the 'need to remain motivated' and then again not to 'become so involved in your job hunt that you lose touch with friends and former colleagues … you need to avoid becoming a hermit.' The big Boss wants you to enjoy freedom but still make sure that you:

> Explain how you overcame whatever situation caused you to take time off. Did you find an added inner strength that you never knew existed? Did you use your time off to learn a new skill that will be of benefit to the job? Unless you spent months on a sofa flicking channels, you're likely to have achieved something during your time off that will impress a new employer so make sure you focus on that area. (Monster 2010b)

The big Boss makes impossible demands upon us. It wants us to be proactive in improving employability while having a life apart, to enjoy life. The ethic of employability, our calling, marks us out as independent but essentially a compromised quantum of capital.

The big Boss is in the ether at an interview, weighing heavy over the interview panel but never settling on to a particular face. It connects what we imagine are the more localised demands of the company and the universal demands of capital. It is there when we clock in and out of work. It probes us with questions about the worth of our labours. We might start to despise him and consider his judgements unfair but he cannot be exorcised. We must remain in contention for jobs, his presence cannot be wished away.

This is no 'autotelic self' that Giddens proselytises. It is not a person who translates 'potential threats into rewarding challenges' and turns 'entropy into a consistent flow of experience' (Giddens 1994:102). Reflexivity is predicated on an anxiety that capital thrives on. The result is a commodification, not liberation, of the self. It is appropriate to call this a *reflexive exploitation*,[14] the ongoing reflection on the self as object of exchange, a kind of ongoing self assessment, the sort of technology that *Records of Achievement* embody. The US Careeer One Stop website (2011) describes self assessments as 'a way to learn about yourself: what you like, what you don't like, and how you tend to react to certain situations ... tools to help you explore your skills, interests, values, or other traits.' This is what happens in reflexive exploitation, a conscious calculation of worth through an often unconscious submission to the language capital has appropriated for its own calling. It appropriates the language of difference, the space of self-determination and the principles and practices that give meaning to life. By extending into the private sphere, the bureaucracy stages its own dissolution.

Ethics

Administered life

Adorno and Horkheimer saw in the enlightenment process a dialectical twist. Rationality and science had enabled humans to manipulate nature and challenge superstitious beliefs, but also provided the tools of domination that destroy the material and ethical foundations of human society. The subject becomes an object of technical rationalisation, quantified, administered and controlled. This Kafkaesque nightmare world of long corridors and hard insect-like shells encasing our desires is not all that it seems, though. The corridors were sometimes playing fields while the hard shells of the bureaucracy could be put on and taken off.

The pyramid is a common visual metaphor for the hierarchy of power said to define a Fordist bureaucracy. By contrast, the post-Fordist 'post-bureaucracy' is often described as 'flat' with no direct line of command, power fragmented into teams, production outsourced and personal life and professional values blurred. It is a concentrated but decentralised form of domination that remains strong but is also shapeless, writes Richard Sennett (2006).[15] The 'network' is the favoured metaphor today.

The network post-bureaucracy is said to replace the 'pyramid' form of bureaucracy, the kind that formalises working relations to exert, according to Merton, 'a constant pressure upon the official to be "methodical, prudent, disciplined."' (1968:252) Max Weber wrote, perhaps a little misleadingly for our twenty-first-century eyes, that the more bureaucracy 'is "dehumanised", the more completely it succeeds in eliminating from official business love, hatred, and all purely personal, irrational, and emotional elements which escape calculation.' (Cited in Whimster 2004:249) Was Weber describing, then, an institution that demanded total obedience and emotional detachment? Bauman tends towards this reading when relating the bureaucracy to the Nazi administration. And as Lasch said, bureaucracies 'discourage enterprise and independent thinking and ... make the individual distrust his own judgement, even in matters of taste' (1984:29). A form of administration said to produce such outcomes is indeed a straw man worth setting fire to. Management gurus such as William Ouchi, author of 1981's *Theory Z*, were enthusiastic firestarters: 'Only the bureaucratic mechanism explicitly says to individuals, "Do not do what you want, do what we tell you because we pay you for it." The bureaucratic mechanism alone produces alienation, anomie and a lowered sense of autonomy.' (cited in Parker 2000:25) On the surface this appears sympathetic to Max Weber's description. But as Paul Du Gay explains, for Weber the bureaucrat does not exist in a moral vacuum nor is she immune to broader social pressures. She retains the capacity to determine when institutional demands exceed the normative standards of society. The role is 'predicated upon an awareness of the irreducible plurality of and frequent incommensurability between passionately held moral ends and thus of the possible costs of pursuing any one of them at the expense of others', writes Du Gay (2000:76).

Jurgen Habermas (1987) was concerned that a bureaucratic system of calculative-instrumental rationality was encroaching into what he called the lifeworld of feelings and non-instrumentalised relationships, actions and emotions. Bauman proposed a reversal of the 'colonisation of the lifeworld' thesis. We see on chat shows and in public discourse generally, he writes, a 'colonisation of the public sphere by issues previously classified as private and unsuitable for public venting.' (2006:70) Today, according to Hartmann and Honneth, there is a 'debordering' and blurring of private life and professional actions (2006:49). Staying with Weber, Boltanski and Chiapello locate the development of the managerial form of capitalist regulation in the value-rational-actions[16] of the protests of the late 1960s. While their study of French management texts situates their argument in a local context, the findings have broader relevance. Their *New Spirit of Capitalism* is arguably the most sophisticated analysis of the employability aesthetic. They argue that the protests of 1968 formed around two central demands: a 'social critique' by trade unions and workers of working conditions and low pay; and an 'artistic critique' by students and intellectuals of the crushing power of institutions over social life, entailing a loss of individual autonomy, self-expression and difference – a kind of one-dimensionality as Herbert Marcuse saw it.

Employers looked for an 'exit strategy' in response to growing pressures for reform in the face of an economic downturn. The first response was to improve pay and working conditions, but a second economic downturn in the mid 1970s meant that capital would have to seek another solution. It turned to the ambiguous demands of students and intellectuals by appealing to the worker as a distinct individual with the capacity for independent thought and initiative. For management gurus Peters and Waterman (1995:234), workers would now be treated as partners, with dignity and respect. The *new* spirit of capitalism relied on a 'sophisticated ergonomics, incorporating the contributions of post-behaviourist psychology and the cognitive sciences' to engage the workforce as psychological entities with individual needs and desires, Boltanski and Chiapello (2007:465) write.

With employers now recognising the personal worth of each individual member of the labour force, new tests were set up to determine whether people actually possessed the valued attributes. Boltanski and Chiapello describe a number of 'justificatory regimes', basically the principles for determining the fairness of an organisational form and the criteria for inclusion into it.[17] They call the dominant justificatory regime today the 'projective city'. Workers are judged by the projects they are involved in and the ongoing connections they make. The projective city is:

> a mass of connections apt to create forms – that is to say, bring objects and subjects into existence – by stabilizing certain connections and making them irreversible. It is thus a temporary *pocket of accumulation* which, creating value, provides a base for the requirement of extending the network by furthering connections. (Boltanski & Chiapello 2007:104)

In basing inclusion into the workforce on the strength of a person's connections, values and activities, the struggle for better pay and conditions is individualised and measured according to the new criteria of personal freedom and enterprise. This would transform relations between workers and management and forces hostile to capitalism would be won over as companies appeal to the character of an individual ego. Elton Mayo recognised how such strategies would undermine trade unions reliant as they are for their organisational power on the collective identity of the workforce.[18] He was one of a number of advocates of a strategy that would make the organisation a standard bearer for the human being in all its diversity and with all its compassion for others.

Business ethics, according to Martin Parker (2003:189), assumes political economy to be a given while leaving open questions about the values and orientations of people. With ethics separated from politics, business can assume the role of guardian of an *a priori* universal truth, the right of individuals to pursue self-interest on the open market. Without the crucial political dimension, demands for a more ethical way of doing business are conceived within a linguistic frame that business can all too easily accede to. It is hard to see, though, how business can be grounded in a political ethics, as Parker proposes, when profit is its underlying motive. A recurrent theme in sections on ethics in *Capitalism's New Clothes* is the competitive benefits to companies that wear the ethical clothes. What are called corporate values serve to deflect flak, incorporate critical discourses and establish connections with the fetishised notions of difference by which individuals are currently conceived. A point also developed in the next chapter is that when objects – corporations, products and so on – assume an ethical status they serve as vessels into which our own ethical concerns can be transferred, taking on the role of ethical actor on our behalf. When working for a company that 'values' the individual, we can feel that a cause greater than profit is served.

Ethical values are the retractable flesh covering the corporate incisors that cut into the human tissue. By appealing to our ethical concerns the company itself takes on the role of a human personality and what it demands in return is a person who shares its values.[19] For example, the UK national charity TimeBank (2010) helps people to develop valuable networks through charitable activities. Their stated aim is in 'inspiring and connecting a new generation of people to volunteer in their communities, and enabling charitable organisations and businesses to develop innovative and effective volunteer recruitment programmes.' So what can volunteering do for you, the website asks,

> Sure, volunteering is great for your community and makes the world a better place; but could it actually make a positive impact on your life, too?
> Whether you want to improve your CV with new skills, meet new people or just feel good about yourself, TimeBank can hook you up with a volunteer opportunity that could change your life for the better. (Timebank 2010)

As one volunteer of the scheme put it, 'It was a real confidence builder, knowing I could think on my feet.'

No pain without gain. By appropriating the hitherto informal networks of social interaction and the value-rational orientations according to which some of us act into its discourse, the rich and colourful textures of human life are turned into instruments of enterprise. This cynically interprets human action as disguised self-interest, providing a rationale for thinking of the self in terms of its CV, a mirror double that lodges into thought the question of whether such and such activity can also, perhaps serendipitously, help with our career goals. It turns reflection into reflexive exploitation.

With the help of Reed Executive, TimeBank carried out a survey to show that among 200 of the UK's leading businesses:

- 73 per cent of employers would employ a candidate with volunteering experience over one without
- 94 per cent of employers believe that volunteering can add to skills
- 58 per cent say that voluntary work experience can actually be more valuable than experience gained in paid employment
- 94 per cent of employees who volunteered to learn new skills had benefited either by getting their first job, improving their salary, or being promoted.

Sound reasons for thinking of the benefits of 'doing' voluntary work.

Marcuse saw labour as a block to the realisation of a society based on pleasure. In our labours we submit to the reality principle of instrumental action, a mode of practice or 'performance principle' peculiar to capitalism. By considering work 'as a machine' and mechanising it accordingly, it is possible, Marcuse wrote, to anticipate in automated technologies 'the *potential* basis of a new freedom for man.' (2002:6) Marcuse, who was considerably influential among the student movements of the late 1960s, is one of the artistic critics Boltanski and Chiapello have in mind. And we can see that in a way management has taken on Marcuse's critique of deadening labour by transforming the workplace as a site that encourages autonomy, self-expression and play. But we should be clear about just how limited this embrace of Marcuse is. The managerial firm omits two crucial conditions for the liberation of 'man' from the performance principle. First, to create the space in which individuals can flourish, working hours would have to be significantly reduced without affecting income. The opposite has in fact happened, as Pietro Basso has shown.[20] Second, pleasure would be liberated from capital, not put to the service of it as has happened. The more we 'express' our identities in our labours the greater it seems is our material impoverishment.

Boltanski and Chiapello appear to share Marcuse's pessimism about the prospect for overcoming alienated labour by proposing, instead of the liberation of the human capacity for creative activity from its materialist constraints, a liberation from the uncertainties of what they call project work. Business, they argue, needs to take responsibility for the employability of the worker by creating opportunities for workers to be involved in projects that enhance employability. Workers need guaranteed 'rights' to employability:

Giving workers the right to employability would go some way to constrain capital, were such a measure introduced. This would be a major concession, from who exactly is unclear given what Boltanski and Chiapello (2007:510) have to say about capitalism: released from control, *without constraints* [my emphasis], capitalism knows no criteria except the private interests of the strongest, and has no reason to take account of the general interest. No 'invisible hand' now intervenes to guide it when the institutions and agreements without which the market cannot function collapse.

Boltanski and Chiapello's reliance on managerial texts, which do not concern themselves with the totality of the system they speak of, may help to explain why they take the view that capitalism is 'unsupervised'.[21] In such a thesis it makes sense to emphasise the dominance of networked forms of power, such as those described by Castells who claims that,

> the network enterprise is neither a network of enterprises nor an intra-firm, networked organisation. Rather, it is a lean agency of economic activity, built around specific business projects, which are enacted by networks of various composition and origin: *the network is enterprise*. (2002:67)

Boltanski and Chiapello would then be right to claim, by this logic, that exploitation is more specifically about the use capital makes of a person's connections.

While business organisations help foster the 'technologies' of self-governance, the state apparatuses remain instrumental in creating the structural frameworks for organisations in general to introduce new methods to control the workforce. Business knows no criterion except the pursuit of profit and so it is left to the state apparatuses to take account of and serve the general interest of capital by acting as mediator between employer and employee. Employability is an ideology promulgated, institutionalised and effectively forced upon the worker in a compact between state and capital.

Just as Hardt and Negri's reading of capitalism leads to a confused, albeit logically consistent, rejection of territorial proletarian struggles in favour of the dispersed struggles of the multitude, so Boltanski and Chiapello's critique of 'connectionist exploitation' leads them to frame struggle in terms of employability rights. If 1968, or for that matter the British miner's strike of 1984–85, was a failed revolution, the ideas that inspired those who fought for the liberation of men and women from their alienated labour were more than this, and their demands are relevant today.

Enjoyment

Happy consciousness revisited

Marcuse described the happy consciousness as someone satisfied that, despite everything, the system delivers the goods. They sacrifice a piece of their freedom to labour and in return earn the privilege to gratify their desires at the shopping mall. Lacan makes a similar point. In this one-dimensional society of enjoyment the superego no longer commands us to repress our desires, say for premarital sex, but rather to enjoy the desire; you must because you can, as Žižek puts it.[22] We saw this play out in the credit-based consumer boom of the last decade. Loans are available to everyone, so there is no excuse not to buy that new kitchen you wanted, and on it goes. And what the kitchen or whatever other object we desire represents is a thing substituted for the thing or *objet petit a* lacking in our selves, the object that Lacan assigns a special quality to. As Žižek explains:

> The ultimate lesson of psychoanalysis is that human life is never 'just life': humans are not simply alive, they are possessed by the strange drive to enjoy life in excess, passionately attached to a surplus which sticks out and derails the ordinary run of things. (2006:61)

The *objet petit a* is the little piece or 'missing' thing we are driven to possess or 'recover'. The crucial point being that 'it' never existed in the first place and if hypothetically we were to somehow obtain it the drive to live beyond mere existence would be exhausted. There are parallels here with Marx's notion of species being, the capacity to refashion nature in our image is 'lost' when put to the service of, and thereby appropriated by the capitalist. The drive to recover this lost object, for self-determination, is part of the history of class struggle and in a Lacanian frame this struggle is never ending. The 'Lacanian' Marx would argue that there is no intrinsic being as such and so alienation is something that can never be overcome or got rid of – essentially Louis Althusser's (2005) reading of the late Marx.

Marx's notion of species being has been criticised for ontologising the human as possessing personal attributes inherent to its biology. The later Marx of commodity fetishism emphasises the fundamental part that people *in their relationships with one another* play in the development of the productive forces. Whether we conceptualise the human capacity to transform nature in its image as inherent to biology or in its social relations is moot. Whatever we think about the way humans are constituted, we are still creative beings by necessity and this deployment is essential to the survival of the species. These are important qualifications, for they allow us – without getting into metaphysical knots – to recognise the centrality of this capacity to our lives, whether we express it through work or not. The importance of having self-determination of this capacity, and the means to express it for the purposes of well-being and society as a whole, cannot be overstated. Whenever I use the term species being, I do so with these qualifications in mind.

Another word for the excessive or surplus-enjoyment Lacan describes is *jouissance*, crudely related to the fleeting pleasure of orgasm.[23] We go to excessive lengths to achieve it and once it happens it is immediately lost. The pleasure lies in the obstacle to fulfilment, always hitting against the limit but never quite getting there – for as soon as we do, the whole process of recovery has to begin over again. Guilt is a resulting emotion, the shame of letting our desires take control of us. And once again we can relate this to Marx, as Lacan does, by comparing *jouissance* or surplus-enjoyment to surplus-value. The boss steals our *jouissance* from us, effectively denying our pleasure as we labour for him, and uses that energy to service his own pleasures. We snatch back a piece of *jouissance* every time we get one over on him. And in a game of pass the parcel, he returns a piece when rewarding us with promotion and when recognising our contributions to the company. In the *Times Best Companies to Work For* survey (2010) 77 per cent of employees at the UK division of Microsoft (ranked 44th overall) 'say that managers regularly express their appreciation when they do a good job.' This little piece of *jouissance* militates against feelings of dissatisfaction with the *objet petit a* holding out the carrot of the better job to come.

While the subject is engaged in a constant struggle to recover its potency on the job market, the capitalist has to work constantly to recover surplus-value. As soon at it makes profit it has to strive to get more. If either the subject or capital could ever be fulfilled, if either possessed the thing that causes desire, there would be no operational motive. Capitalism hits against its limit in crises of overaccumulation and it is this danger, counter-intuitively perhaps, that revitalises capitalism, as Boltanski and Chiapello argue.

But according to Lacan, Marx understood surplus-value as a quantity of capital directly used by the embodied capitalist for his own personal fulfilments. It follows in Lacan's reading of Marx that if profit goes back into the accumulative process, as was always the case in fact, the capitalist too is accordingly 'exploited' by the nonexistent object of his libidinal desire, the desire to expand and thereby make additional profits. Let us say, then, that capitalists and proletarians are exploited by their own libidinal desires for an object neither can fully possess. For capitalists that object is profit and for the proletariat that object is employability. The difference, and it is a crucial one, is that employability as the object of proletarian desire is linguistically and materially determined by capital. It is linguistically determined insofar that the boss, conditioned by the orthodoxies of a particular mode of regulation, assumes the power to signify what employability actually means. It is materially determined insofar that the subject who strives for employability does so only in order to be materially exploited by capital. In this way capitalist *jouissance* (for surplus-value) is knotted with proletarian *jouissance* (for material security). Employability becomes the master signifier of this knot.

This knotting of desires in regard to employment has parallels with the knotting of desires in regard to consumption. In the latter, the 'consumer' enjoys the thing that keeps capital in circulation, the products and services it has created. While we might identify ourselves as consumers, work is the means for earning a wage to enable us to consume. The knot of capital and labour, quilted in the concept of employability, is what binds linguistic desire to material capital.

Exploitation and alienation is then two fold. First, in a Marxist sense, the actual capitalist who employs us materially exploits us. He takes our creative capacities from us, our labour power, and makes use of them for his own gain. Concrete labour becomes labour in the abstract. Our desires are also exploited, in a Lacanian sense, by our own libidinal investments in becoming the object of the *imagined* capitalist, our future boss who could be the next employer or our current boss whose future desires we anticipate for the purposes of promotion. Whereas Marxists typically focus on material exploitation, to understand the nature of our exploitation in the labour market today we *also* need a concept of the latter libidinal exploitation, derived here from Lacan. But we should be clear. If we conceive of exploitation only as Lacan understands it and of alienation simply as a linguistic separation, we miss the crucial point, as so many 'post' Marxists do, that the site of power, where the capacity to signify what it means to be employable resides, is a material phenomenon and in this sense *real* not imagined. The 'capitalist' is also real. He is embodied in the owners and gatekeepers – managers, principal shareholders, political figures and so on – of the mode of production.

The material and linguistic forms of separation, respectively defining Marx and Lacan's concepts of alienation, are dual features of the subjective relation to the labour market. Moreover, because the symbolic form of employability – standing in as the object cause of desire, always lost and never possessed – is the thing we must strive to possess in order to satisfy material needs, language is also material. This brings us closer to the material linguistics of Mikhail Bakhtin and V.N. Volosinov, the latter explaining that:

> In order for any item, from whatever domain of reality it may come, to enter the social purview of the group and elicit ideological semiotic reaction, it must be associated with the vital socioeconomic prerequisites of the particular group's existence; it must somehow, even if only obliquely, make contact with the bases of the group's material life. (1973:22)

Rather than go down that path, I want to remain with Lacan whose account of subjective drives and desires is of richer importance to this analysis. In the ideal bureaucracy of capitalism, desire is entangled in the two ideologically distinct but practically reinforcing spheres of work and leisure. At work we enjoy self-sacrifice in the higher calling of the work ethic. In leisure, following Adorno and Horkheimer, we enjoy the objects the culture industry provides. In the ideal managerial form of capitalism the ideology is entangled in a different way. The subject sacrifices herself to the command 'be yourself', the call to self-determination which becomes a commodified object of exchange when 'being yourself' translates as a value employers seek; alienation in Marx's sense becomes a commodity (see below). Consider the UK law firm Pannone (2010): 'We expect everyone who joins us to enjoy working hard but also to have a life outside work!' Work and leisure remain ideologically distinct and practically reinforcing; here, however, the ethic of work is reformulated as an ethic of employability extending beyond the workplace in space and in time. Insofar that employability is a thing we are compelled to pursue at work and outside of it, the bureaucracy stretches to encompass all of life. As such, the formal freedom the bureaucrat enjoyed becomes an informal freedom, the bluff of the capitalist who tells us to submit to our desires and in doing so chart a path to the law of surplus-value, another way of saying the subject is a self-interested rational actor. Such power goes unrecognised. We become falsely conscious of the fact that he is the master because, in our private existence where we cultivate our CVs, the connection to abstract labour (the power of labour embodied in the production process) is obscured by employability as the 'decentred' Lacanian form of exploitation proper to capitalism today.

A cynic might say, 'of course I recognise how I am ensnared into this relation so I perform the role without actually believing in it.' But what she does not recognise is that the very distance she imagines lies between herself and what the company demands of her is the separation that companies such as Pannone demand. I return to this later.

Enjoyment is an obligation to be our selves, spontaneity is instrumentalised and the CV functions like a passport stamped with the sign of enterprise.

Human aesthetic

Freud located the socialising authority in the parent. Adorno and Horkheimer located it in the mass media using the term 'extra-familial' socialisation. Lacan said that the superego now commands us to enjoy, but always within the symbolic frame of society. The difference with the big Boss is that when it threatens castration – unemployment, low status jobs and so on – for not keeping up with his demands, he threatens our very livelihood. When he shows us how to behave and provides clues as to what it means to be employable, we have to take note. Yet on the surface the world appears like an open canvas upon which an autonomous subject can paint her colours. The bureaucracy today, Žižek explains,

> not only reduces the subject to its mouthpiece, but also wants the subject to disavow the fact that he is merely its mouthpiece and to (pretend to) act as an autonomous agent – a person with a human touch and personality, not just a faceless bureaucrat. The point, of course, is not only that such an autonomisation is doubly false, since it involves a double disavowal, but also that there is no subject prior to the Institution (prior to language as the ultimate institution): subjectivity is produced as the void in the very submission of the life-substance of the Real to the Institution. (2000:259)

Deleuze and Guattari make a similar point in their book on Franz Kafka. The bureaucracy, they say, is an assemblage of desires, like gears in a technical machine, 'that brings into coexistence engineers and parts, materials and machined personnel, executioners and victims, the powerful and the powerless' (1986:57). For them, desire is a flow of differing intensities forming into temporary assemblages or creations; the bureaucracy is one such creation. But while desiring flows are captured in repressive assemblages, they are never entirely contained within them; there is always the possibility to exceed the coordinates of any machine of capture. The managerial firm codifies the intensities of desire that Deleuze and Guattari saw as 'virtual lines of flight' or escape. It factors escape into production. The non-administered excess of time and space are the sites where ideas are accumulated, generic skills developed and a personality rounded. The human is a becoming-machine-of-capital. Consider the following advice from a graduate career directory:

> [A]s well as anticipating their [employer's] criteria you must also make the human signals ... Show confidence, smile, be natural and enthusiastic. The ideal candidate demonstrates impeccable preparation and comes across as human too. (Prospects 2010)

The technologies of self-governance are deployed to shape and guide individuals on how to become human. Like a guitar string that has to be tuned up to E, we have to work up to becoming human. Prior to this the worker has no substance. Without the signals that convey our humanity we are the unemployable bare life, to use Georgio Agamben's term (1995), neither dead nor alive on unemployment and incapacity benefits.

Bauman (1997) differentiated between a tourist choosing where to go and who to meet from the stranger trapped in her world. In this 'two nations'-in-one-space the 'oppressed have been denied the resources for identity-building and so (for all practical intents and purposes) also the tools of citizenship' (Bauman 1997:34). Appropriating this for our purposes, the not employable subject is proto-human, unformed but with a capacity, under the right conditions and with the will, to become the human of capital.

Employment agencies provide the tools for identity building by signposting on the tourist's/worker's itinerary the forking paths of possibility, some of which are dead ends, others of which are hazardous and the best of which promise exceptional views. The worker has no choice other than to choose a pathway and discover her identity along the way, the identity that the big Boss signifies as belonging to the human, and thus avoid becoming the stranger.

Subjectivity is defined and constituted in the lexicon of employability. The Career Energy jobs website shows us the way. By becoming enthusiastic, in this example, we signify our humanness. Enthusiasm, they say, is:

> [T]he *art* of making other people feel positive because you are *seen* to be positive. An enthusiastic team member *appears* to be glad to be doing their job, is better placed to override obstacles and minimise conflict. People enjoy being around an enthusiastic person and enthusiasm will *boost your standing* in the eye of your colleagues and bosses. It is *hard to display enthusiasm externally* unless you are enthusiastic *internally*. But even if you do not enjoy your job, it is possible, with the right support, to *develop and demonstrate* an enthusiasm for it. [My emphasis throughout] (Freedman 2009)

On a superficial reading this quotation seems contradictory, but it makes sense if we approach it dialectically as a 'negation of the negation' of identity.

In the first negation, words such as 'art', 'seen', 'appears' and 'display' tell us that emotion is something that has to be manufactured, conforming to the psychoanalytic view that, anxiety aside, human emotions are fake. In the first place, prior to the job, we are subjects without substance: the proto-human. The truth is told; there is no authentic core to subjectivity. In the second negation, we develop and demonstrate enthusiasm by covering over the lack of subjectivity by becoming human capital. If business does not recognise the particular character, emotion, activity, value, attitude and so on, as belonging to the firm, then that person does not exist for them. As Marx would see it, the proletarian is a subject without substance because capital has taken the substance from her. Those who wear the mask of employability are the substance processed by and for capital.

The first step to becoming human involves thinking about the self as an appearance. The image is an appropriation of what the big Boss wants. Inverting Arlie Hochschild's (2003) emotional labour thesis. Here, the false smile (appearance) is the predicate for the genuine one (reality). The smile is not ours to give but to acquire. So unpacking this:

1. The feeling is recognised as an object.
2. A technique for mimicking the feeling is learnt.
3. A mask is worn.
4. Because there is nothing beneath the mask, the mask itself becomes the genuine expression of feeling.
5. Enthusiasm is for real.

The unformed raw material from which the smile is created is mined from the untapped resources of everyday life. The commodity value of the raw emotion, the 'cocoa', is low and the commodity value of the processed emotion, the 'chocolate', is high. Now let us return to Marx's notion of alienated labour.

Alienation as a commodity

Marx distinguishes the human species, within a socio-historical context, by its capacity to observe and transform nature and itself through material and mental production. This creative capacity comes to represent an alienated object when put to the service of capital and so we are deprived of our substance, our species being. By having power over labour, capital also has power to signify what constitutes subjectivity. Alienation is both material and linguistic and in both cases the proletariat is an eviscerated subordinate of capital. Bakhtin and Volosinov understood this when situating language within its historical material context; every utterance is an echo of the past resonating in the present and refracting the future.

Where we need to go beyond Marx, however, is in recognising that the worker consciously identifies itself as an alienated object by looking outside of the paid relation for expressions of genuine emotion, and finding there resources that can help it cope with, and enter into, employment. It discovers its humanity by retreating from labour, which it often sees as alienating, and by having a life outside of labour to develop resources into it. Alienation becomes a commodity.

Free time is a space in which value is accrued for the production of an employable subjectivity. It is also the space in which the individual misrecognises herself as a self-determining subject: she does not see how the object of desire, the imagined perfect job, exploits her. Adorno had understood this misrecognition. The 'human condition', he wrote, 'which sees itself as the opposite of reification, the oasis of unmediated life within a completely mediated total system, has itself been reified just like the rigid distinction between labour and free time.' (2001:189) Free time is also a site where human use-values are produced.

Adorno is often charged with regarding consumers as dupes of the culture industry whose products it laps up in dull rhythmic conformity. But his main point is that the exchange-value of culture has supplanted its use-value, that in fact what we enjoy, evocative of Marx's notion of commodity fetishism, is exchange itself. Moreover, for Adorno,

> People are not only, as the saying goes, falling for the swindle; if it guarantees them even the most fleeting gratification *they desire a deception which is nonetheless transparent to them*. They force their eyes shut and voice approval, in a kind of self-loathing, for what is meted out to them, knowing fully the purpose for which it is manufactured. [emphasis added] (2001:103)

It is not for lack of knowledge that we are seduced into wanting the thing. Many of those who read Dan Brown's *The Da Vinci Code*, for example, have a fair idea that it is no masterpiece of prose fiction. It is because we are savvy to the ploy that we permit ourselves to consume the product without feeling we have been duped into buying it. Awareness of the product's inferiority helps to sell it because then we can knowingly enjoy it without feeling we have been duped. Peter Sloterdijk describes such an attitude as enlightened false-consciousness:

> It is the universally widespread way in which enlightened people see to it that they are not taken for suckers. There even seems to be something healthy in this attitude, which, after all, the will to self-preservation generally supports. It is the stance of the people who realise that the times of naïveté are gone. (2008:5)

The deodorant brand Lynx runs a series of advertisements satirising the sex appeal of perfumed products. In them we see a young male who after spraying Lynx onto his skin is chased by a group of attractive women. The obvious message is that Lynx equals sex appeal. In its exaggerated way, though, the advert decodes the message for us. The cynic sees past the surface only to be duped into thinking he is savvy to the obvious ploy. While it is possible to resist interpellation as a sexy individual, it is impossible to resist interpellation as savvy. Knowing the ruse only makes us savvy to the ruse and being savvy makes us sexy. There is no way out of this. However enlightened we are, we are still savvy. The enlightened among us are the ones who are cultural dupes *and* know it. We see past the surface only to arrive back at the same point we thought we could escape, that of our symbolic interpellation as sexy/savvy. The cynic who thinks he sees past the trick is the least aware of how trapped he is. Relating this to employment, by not identifying herself in her actual labour, the worker is *falsely* conscious of the centrality of labour to her existence and sense of who she is. The point, Žižek explains,

> is not just that we must unmask the structural mechanism which is producing the effect of subject as ideological misrecognition, but that we must at the same time fully acknowledge this misrecognition as unavoidable – that is, we must accept a certain delusion as a condition of our historical activity, of assuming a role as agent of the historical process. (1989:2)

What we often fail to realise is that in disidentifying from our labours we are performing the function the employer wants from us. First, the worker does not identify herself as a machine. She is not duped into seeing herself in the image of post-Fordist firms, which according to Andre Gorz's literal reading of organisational desire ask us:

> to give up everything – to give up any other form of allegiance, their personal interests and even their personal life – in order to *give themselves*, body and soul, to the company which, in exchange, will provide them with an identity, a place, a personality and a job they can be proud of. (1999:36)

Second, the worker does the job while identifying herself in a place outside of the role. Her personality is not tied to the company and so her identity does not depend on employment in it. She is savvy to the demand and has a life outside of the job (what the employer essentially demands). Third, she is naive in regarding this knowledge as evidence of not being beholden to the employer, that objectively she is not a worker as Marx understood the term. If one disidentifies from their labour, there is no need for militant action in the workplace because better pay and working conditions are achievable by improving employability and getting a different job. The struggle is therefore displaced on to an individualistic quest for employability. In such a way, the ontological investment in the job is reduced and along with it the struggle for better pay and working conditions. However, the work ethic is still in demand: employers note that applicants 'lack presentation skills, teamwork skills, and overall interpersonal (e.g., gets along well with others) skills. Employers also note that new grads [sic] tend to lack a good work ethic.' (JobWeb 2010) It is just that the desire for employability takes the worker beyond their immediate role into the fantasy realm of independence from capital, a grandiose vision of a future foretold and always delayed. It is a work ethic by other means.

Fleming and Sewell misidentify 'flannelling', the mocking overidentification of workers with company policies, as a form of resistance (2002:866). Workers are not subverting capital by mocking it. Providing she completes the task in an efficient manner the worker's labour power is put to good use. Although the company may have correctly been identified as the exploiter, unless ways are found to negate surplus-value the worker is still useful to the firm. This savvy worker is not the automaton. But she is falsely conscious of how she works to make herself into a machine of capital without ever fully becoming one. In disidentifying from her boss she becomes fully flexible in the labour market.

The word disidentification implies a consciousness of oneself as distinct from a particular identifiable thing. Beverley Skeggs (2005) describes a 'disidentification and dissimulation' of certain women in their attempts not to be recognised as working class and their struggles to assume the imagined symbolic codes of the middle classes. When a person jokes about how ridiculous they look when wearing a suit to an interview they disidentify from the role being performed. However, this, according to Žižek, is a case of false disidentification. Whatever we think about the thing we do and however we choose to reflect upon it, we are still after all doing it. As Žižek writes, '[W]e perform our symbolic mandates without assuming them and "taking them seriously"' (2002:70). Christopher Lasch (1991) earlier described the same phenomenon as a banal pseudo-self-awareness.

False disidentification is ontologically decentring. We do the job but we identify ourselves in a place outside of it in either space or time. In a spatial sense, we identify with the interests, pastimes and activities that take place outside of work, evenings, weekends and holidays. In a temporal sense, we identify with an imagined future job when our talents will we hope be recognised and rewarded. In each case our true self is imagined to reside outside and beyond the current job. In this way the worker maintains a false distance from the actual labour and so, whatever happens at work, she is able to maintain a stable sense of who she is because the insecure job has not defined her. Because our identity traverses and transcends our labour we are better equipped psychically to cope with disappointment in our labours.

Take, as an example, a struggling artist. She supports her passion by working in a call centre for a significant proportion of her week. Though the work of answering phones is monotonous and unfulfilling, her passion for art and belief in her ability to succeed as an artist make the job bearable. She identifies as an artist first and foremost. Her investments are displaced both spatially and temporally. Her identity is solid in its displacement: not liquid, frozen not fluid; she identifies as a worker insofar that she describes art as her work. She is exploited by the object of her desire to be a professional artist and by the employer whose dominance over her is obscured, so any antagonism towards the firm is defused because she has no interest in pursuing a future there. She maintains a work ethic, but a work ethic resignified as an aesthetic of employability.

On the other hand, a cleaning worker who feels content with her role does not identify herself in a future role and so is insufficiently enterprising to improve employability to succeed in other roles. A person can also falsely identify with a conferred status. For example, a graduate on a casual lecturing contract prescribed the label of lecturer, and valued by students as the possessor of desired knowledge, falsely identifies as master. In such examples, the imagined self-identity is sustained by the recognition the actual job affords. The university that employs her becomes the effective mount that holds the imagined ego in place. Such a path should be signified as 'hazardous' when permanent jobs in academia are so hard to come by. The identity, while centred on the workplace, is here identification with a *future* position. Knowing this, the worker, flattered by the status conferred on her, is indebted to the employer who allows her to enjoy the status – to enjoy her role as symptomatic of labour market deregulation – and who promises a more secure job in the future. Her vulnerability coupled with her imagined identity makes her more exploitable.

Some practical considerations

Unlike Hardt and Negri, who make no distinction between exploitation in the workplace and exploitation of subjectivity in every facet of life, in my argument there are two distinctive but mutually reinforcing spheres of exploitation, each with distinctive and overlapping properties. Outside of paid labour, 'clocked off time', there is no direct exploitation of labour power, so the unemployed, for example, are not exploited (in a Marxist sense). It is only when 'clocked in' to work that a person can be said to be contributing to surplus-value, or perhaps not if the firm is loss making. By clocked in we should mean any activity that is commissioned by and enacted for the employer and remunerated for the time, quantity of output, profitable outcomes, or, more indirectly, as the additional unmeasured service one commits to the employer while working for them, unpaid overtime, conference attendance, entertaining clients and so on. The exploitation that occurs in clocked-off time can be divided between its spatial and temporal components in which exploitation occurs in a Lacanian sense: the subject is exploited by the object of their own libidinal desire, with the important qualification that the object in question for the purposes of this argument is the phantasmal better job (employability). This connects Lacanian exploitation with exploitation in Marx: the object of desire is the desire to be exploited by a future real boss. We can put this another way, this time through John Holloway's distinction between doing and abstract labour.

John Holloway evokes Marcuse to argue that a struggle against capitalism necessarily entails a struggle against not only abstract labour, the combined material and mental creative faculties of human life that are put to the service of surplus-value, but also concrete labour, the useful non-alienated component of human activity that precedes its transmogrification into surplus or exchange-value. Whereas abstract labour reduces all human activity, life and expression to an exchange relation transforming all social relations in the process, concrete labour still denotes human activity according to its (instrumental) usefulness in the productive process. The implication of conceiving struggle as one of control of labour is that everything comes down to a confrontation between workers and capitalists at the site of production. Victory would transform the relations of production but not the forces of production. The forces of production include the machinery and labour as an abstract quantity that goes into making things. Postone (2003), whom Holloway cites, makes the argument that in a social revolution it is not simply the relations of production (between capitalist and worker) that changes, but the forces too (our actual labour). In China, for example, the relations of production changed after the revolution, but the forces of production were modelled on the western capitalist form which helps explain how it was so easy for China to become the 'factory of the world' today.

Holloway (2010:99) proposes that instead of concrete labour we should be talking about concrete doing which he defines as 'the ecstasy of abstract labour: ecstacy as ek-stasis [sic.], standing outside of abstract labour while existing within it, standing outside as actual and potential otherness.' Concrete doing is therefore excessive to capital; it is surplus to surplus-value. He lists many examples of concrete doing, anything from reading a book in the park, playing guitar in a band, encouraging students to read Marx, or even taking up arms to fight injustice in Mexico. These are what he calls 'cracks' in capitalism, fissures or spaces that open up and out of which we can identify the potential for change when that potential seems all but lost in the workplace.

Deleuze's critique of struggles centred on the workplace is sympathetic to Holloway's crack capitalism thesis. To recap, Deleuze claimed that we have entered into societies of control in which there are no established boundaries or territorial limits of power, a world of individuals reduced to a numerical form, data or 'dividual', where anything from the quality of childcare to teaching is evaluated and audited. Deleuze adds that many young people now embrace the brash rivalries that are being encouraged. They 'strangely boast of being "motivated"; they re-request apprentice-ships and permanent training' (Deleuze 1992:37). Trade unions, he says, are designed to respond to disciplinary powers with their identifiable spaces of enclosure: the factory, prison, university, and so on. With corporate power and marketing uncoiling serpent-like across networks new forms of resistance are needed, and this is precisely what Holloway is claiming.

Of course, Holloway recognises that reading a book does not have the same implication as taking up arms. He also recognises, unlike Hardt and Negri, that class struggle remains central in the fight against abstract labour. The difference with my argument is that he sees these doings as 'standing outside capitalist labour, a projection against and beyond my [worker] entrapment within abstract labour' (2010:99), whereas I have argued that the outside of labour is a source of value into labour, because capital recognises the value in what happens outside of labour. And this is the problem. If abstract labour is the source of value, as I and many others including Holloway would argue, then struggle must be collective and directed against surplus-value and only then, once we are free from abstract labour, can we conceive of being in any way liberated from labour. The cracks are signs of what a future without capital could look like. Cracks are crucial, therefore, to inspire us into fighting for a different kind of society. Regardless of their value to capital, they are also means by which we derive satisfactions without which life would be intolerable. Furthermore, in agreement with Holloway, the effect of our actions at a micro-level cannot be known in advance, although certain actions are more likely to achieve a greater impact than others. So, although my argument is that alienation is a commodity into labour, there is a dialectical aspect to this insofar that the 'concrete doings' are only potentially valuable to capital and can under certain circumstances, *in combination with other people's 'doings'*, negatively affect surplus appropriation.

So what I am not arguing, therefore, is that concrete doing is unimportant and without potential. If I thought otherwise there would be little point or satisfaction for me in trying to and sometimes succeeding in inspiring students to develop their critical thought, interest in and capacity to take part in political struggle. If students produce better essays as a consequence then the boss is also satisfied and my pedagogical reputation improves along with my employability. Not only is it self-destructive to resist employability, it is also destructive to colleagues and those who depend on the services we provide if, cynically, we distance ourselves from our labours. There is nothing intrinsically problematic in possessing a work ethic. Employability is a concept, however signified, that we are stuck with. Struggling against employability is therefore reactive if it affects our non-instrumental dedication to those whose lives we can have a positive impact on through our actions at work and outside of it. But these sorts of struggles, the 'cracks', pose no apparent threat to surplus-value and are not therefore political in a meaningful way. It is only when we act to improve our employability within a collective struggle – that is, when we struggle collectively to obtain the object that causes desire – that we threaten to extinguish once-and-for-all the boss's desire. In short, to have social self-determination over our lives and our labours means being in possession of the means to signify employability.

Conclusion

In this chapter, I have argued that employability is the empty signifier of the boss's desire. We make ourselves likeable by producing a subjectivity that identifies us as human capital. This derives from our capacity to mine ourselves for use-values that are processed and marketed, according to their value, for the purposes of exchange. Temporal and spatial forms of disidentification allow for the production of an identity that capital wants and labour relies on to support its ego-orientations. Alienation from labour becomes a commodity into labour. These displacements of identity defuse a political character the identity might otherwise possess.

The more we chase employability, the more our satisfactions are thwarted and the more we enjoy the mini triumphs that enhance CVs and appear to bring us closer to the object of desire – the ideal, satisfying, secure and impossible non-alienated labour. The only way to escape the employer's signification is to achieve this impossible goal of non-alienated labour by exhausting capital's drive for the object of its desire, the surplus-value. The point is not to resist the desire for employability as this would simply lead to unemployment. Instead, we should fully embrace our desire as our own cause but *also* strive for the object collectively in whichever way we can. By recognising that language is materially situated in the context of employability, we invoke the possibility of overcoming alienation in language in respect of employment. By taking possession of the means to determine what employability means we become master.

A common recognition of how we are exploited by our libidinal desire for employability as a materially determined concept is needed in order for us to develop new strategies to resist capital and take over the role of signifying agent. Employability connects all employers as a single desiring entity called capitalism, the same thing that connects all of us, regardless of our labour, as workers. By wearing the mask of the proletariat the Emperor becomes vulnerable, his nakedness exposed and the thing that drives desire is materialised.

4

NAKED ETHICS

The commodity, once celebrated, has now lost something of its shine. Instead of the mantra 'greed is good' there are numerous 'talking heads', or what Antonio Gramsci called organic intellectuals, raising concerns about the material effects of the system on people and planet. The evident concerns of prominent sociologists about climate change, inequality or even state violence are part of a wider media discourse that we see in television documentaries such as *Blood, Sweat and Tee-Shirts* about child labour in India, high profile campaigns of NGOs and news coverage on anything from poverty in Africa to the devastation wrought by natural phenomena increasingly linked to climate change. Fredric Jameson once said that 'the underside of culture is blood, death, torture and horror.' (1993:5) Today, this is the surface of ideology and what I refer to as a social logic in which socio-material issues are privileged over the cultural-linguistic ones Jameson described as a cultural logic. In their ethical character, these two logics appear to correspond to the progressive demands of leftists. Boltanski and Chiapello identified in the artistic demands of the late 1960s the roots of managerial ideology. The form I describe as today's social logic has no obvious correspondence in organised labour. The ideological driver is a complex of movements, organisations and so on, involving politicians, business leaders, celebrities and a depoliticised public that together operationalise and invoke an ethical injunction to act in response to the image of crisis corresponding to capitalism's new ethical clothes.

In a critical essay on tolerance, Herbert Marcuse distinguished revolutionary from reactionary violence. They are both 'inhuman and evil', he said, but history is never made by ethical standards; the choice is between a violence practised by the oppressed and a violence practised by the oppressor. In the advanced centres of civilisation, he wrote, violence,

> is practiced by the police, in the prisons and mental institutions, in the fight against racial minorities; it is carried, by the defenders of metropolitan freedom, into the backward countries. This violence indeed breeds violence. But to refrain from violence in the face of vastly superior violence is one thing, to renounce a priori violence against violence, on ethical or psychological grounds (because it may antagonise sympathisers) is another. Non-violence is normally not only preached to but exacted from the weak. (Cited in Wolff, et al. 1969:116)

The *a priori* moral foundation of society reflects the established ideology of liberal-parliamentary capitalism. Such universality defines itself against that which it cannot in a given point in time include: illegal immigrants, exploited workers and so on. Liberal ethics, then, is the distorted symbolic form of this underlying Real. Alain Badiou describes contemporary ethics as 'a tourist's fascination for the diversity of morals, customs and beliefs.' (2002:26) If what we recognise as ethics is simply what has already been accepted as legitimate in law then every act that challenges that law is constituted as evil. Ethics takes place from the point of the exception or non-symbolised Real. As Badiou explains, the 'real may be encountered, manifested, or constructed, but it is not represented.' (2007:10) The presence of the real is the truth that every claim to universality elides and every order depends on.

The ethical act, Žižek writes, operates against the totality of a system with its 'symptoms', antagonisms and inconsistencies, including the 'false conflict' between liberalism and fundamentalism (2009:76). The act proper re-writes the subject by changing and temporarily eclipsing the symbolic substance of its identity, an identity described in the previous chapter as one oriented to the demands of employers. The ethical act is therefore, according to Žižek, 'always a "crime", a "transgression" – of the limits of the symbolic community to which I belong.' (2003:83) As with Badiou, ethics takes place in the Real of the exception, always at odds with the social field of 'ethical dilemmas', cultural ethics, environmental ethics and so on, that restrict ethical practice, Alenka Zupančič (2003:95) explains.[1]

When power struggles are reduced to decisions over which party is best able to serve 'the market', we are in the territory of what a number of commentators have called post-politics. Ethics today is recognisable by its absence. What stands today for ethical practice is what Adorno and Horkheimer (1997) and Žižek call pseudo-activity, in essence the doing something, actions that register discontent, without in any way disrupting the symbolic order. An ethics that counts for more than confirmation of existing law is absent and in its absence capitalism appropriates ethical clothes. With the foreclosure of politics proper that we associate with the Left, it is no wonder that, as Jameson (2003:73) puts it, 'It is easier to imagine the end of the world than to imagine the end of capitalism.'

We are called upon today to live with (resignation), adapt to (pro-action), compensate for (care) or change (pseudo-activity) society. We question the 'free-market', the power of corporations and the wars of aggression in Iraq and Afghanistan. Politicians and businessmen lead the way. Five months after the collapse of Lehman Brothers investment bank, the then Prime Minister Gordon Brown told us what we knew already, that,

> Laissez-faire has had its day. People on the centre-left and the progressive agenda should be confident enough to say that the old idea that the markets were efficient and could work things out by themselves are gone. (Cited in Wintour & Watt 2009)

Whereas for the 'post-political' Blair there was no alternative to the market, Brown, who 'accepts full responsibility' for the crisis, linguistically de-naturalises and repoliticises the economy as a territory of state. But the determinable locus of the crisis is rendered indeterminate by an ideology, promulgated on the left, that decentres the capitalist laws of motion by expanding the circumference of possible causes of crises with all their manifest symptoms. In the phase of end-capitalism – in the metacrises of economy and ecology – the potential for inventing causes multiplies. From a chain of causal equivalents the subject decides, with the help of popular media, which cause is most sympathetic to their ideological orientation. This is how the social logic operates and, as we shall see, such logic serves both a political and commercial function.

This chapter is about the ethical principles that corporations, political leaders, celebrities and NGOs have helped, both directly and indirectly, to universalise, commercialise and depoliticise. It is about the way a left-liberal ideology, for want of better term, has been institutionalised to the extent of becoming a general ethical injunction calling into being a subject who acts on the image of their own post-political impotency.

Once again the chapter is organised into three sections on ethics, enterprise and enjoyment.

Ethics

The cultural logic of left-liberalism

In specific periods of time in Western societies, a more pronounced accent is placed on matters of cultural-linguistic concern than on social-materialist ones. A cultural logic, identified with postmodern ideology, centres on notions of recognition, tolerance and so on. Such a politics reifies group identities, exaggerates difference and creates imagined points of antagonism both within and outside the groups being represented. As Nancy Fraser (2000:112) writes, 'The overall effect is to impose a single, drastically simplified group-identity which denies the complexity of people's lives, the multiplicity of their identifications and the cross-pulls of their various affiliations.' Recognition always returns to the question of who does the recognising and according to whose criterion recognition is gained. Appeals for recognition by subaltern groups *de facto* recognise and legitimate the powers that hitherto excluded them. When cultural and economic forms of exclusion are recognised within discourses that aim towards this end, there is no escaping the fact that, however preferable it is to be part of an insider group, the terms for inclusion are made to favour the body that does the recognising. As Agamben remarked:

> It is almost as if, starting from a certain point, every decisive political event were double-sided: the spaces, the liberties, and the rights won by individuals in their conflicts with central powers always simultaneously prepared a tacit but increasing inscription of individuals' lives within the state order, thus offering a new and more dreadful foundation for the very sovereign power from which they wanted to liberate themselves. (Agamben 1995:121)

In its crudest form the politics of recognition flatten out the injuries suffered by different groups, turning material and cultural issues into matters of equivalence.[2] Racial and gender inequality circulates alongside debates on the right of gay men to enter the clergy while those defined illegal in law because of where they were born – immigrants, in other words – have the discourse of recognition pulled from under their territorially-situated feet. There is a fundamental difference between an identity that is chosen and one that is branded onto the body by an external authority.

If recognition is about challenging institutional practices that exclude people on the basis of their cultural identity, their race, gender or ethnicity, tolerance is about policing one's own prejudices towards recognised group identities. Marcuse noted two forms of administrative tolerance; passive toleration of 'entrenched and established ideas' whatever their social effects; and active, official tolerance granted to a spectrum of parties and movements, which he called non-partisan 'abstract' or 'pure' tolerance (Wolff, et al. 1969:108). With abstract tolerance, sense and non-sense are tolerated on the basis that 'nobody, neither group nor individual, is in possession of the truth and capable of defining what is right, wrong, good and bad.' Tolerance cannot be objective and at the same time impartial because 'if truth is more than a matter of logic and science, then this kind of objectivity is false, and this kind of tolerance inhuman.' Against 'repressive tolerance', Marcuse proposed a practice of liberating tolerance or discriminating intolerance; in short, intolerance of movements of the Right and tolerance of movements of the Left (Wolff, et al. 1969).

Echoing Žižek, quoted in Chapter 2 on the politics proper of the Right, George Monbiot wrote a piece in the *Guardian* newspaper arguing that the right-wing Tea Party in the US could teach the left about how to conduct politics. The right, he observes, ruthlessly pursue their objectives, taking no hostages, while the left are effete and ineffectual. He writes (2010), 'the left on both sides of the Atlantic has proved to be tongue-tied, embarrassed, unable to state simple economic truths, unable to name and confront the powers that oppress the working class. It has left the field wide open to rightwing demagogues.' The kind of ruthlessness missing on the left is the discriminating intolerance Marcuse spoke of.

Wendy Brown's critique of tolerance is attuned to the sort of problems we see in the politics of recognition. 'The call for tolerance, the invocation of tolerance, and the attempt to instantiate tolerance', she writes, 'are all signs of identity production and identity management in the context of orders of stratification or marginalisation in which the production, the management, and the context themselves are disavowed.' (2006:14) Brown recognises tolerance as a post-political discourse. However, any attempt within the horizon of capitalism to address the problems Brown rightly identifies would also disappear into what she calls the 'buried order of politics.'

Liberals can be credited for challenging prejudices against minority groups and creating anti-discriminatory laws that help remove institutional barriers to work and welfare provision. It begets, however, what Mooers calls a 'dialectics of embodiment', that ascribes racial, ethnic, sexual and gender profiles to the subject while simultaneously abstracting 'the concrete, sensuous, embodied aspects of human labour.' (2005:34) Badiou (2009) describes this ideology as democratic materialism based, he says, on two sovereign principles. First, we are all material-bodily equivalents with the freedom to define our bodies according to whatever term fits our sense of cultural identity. Second, as repositories of language, bodies become articulations of desire policed by 'linguistic interdictory or stimulating legislations'.

Humanity becomes 'an overstretched vision of animality' (Badiou 2009:34) in which, the world, as Adorno earlier put it, 'becomes the only ideology, and mankind, its component.' (2007:274)

The social logic of left-liberalism

If the cultural logic is the ideological superstructural component of neo-liberalism, the social logic concerns the reproduction of images of destruction wrought by neo-liberalism; these are used by a complex of organisations and individuals to promote an ethical identity and legitimate their privileged social standing. It is a left-liberal ideology that holds no particular agent to account for the many images of poverty, violence, oppression and ecological destruction. It thereby deterritorialises the cause by rejecting the dialectical antagonisms internal to capitalism. In reality, we live, breathe, work, consume and suffer. Yet the Real, Žižek explains apropos of Lacan, is the 'inexorable "abstract" spectral logic of Capital which determines what goes on in social reality' (2001:15), therefore never fully accounted for.

The subject declaring that the system, however conceived, is 'Not in My Name', stages a disidentification every bit as impotent as the employee mocking the company it works for. Corporations, politicians and public professionals get in on the act by declaring a solidarity in the universal struggle for a 'fairer', more 'inclusive' and 'sustainable' society. The new clothes of capitalism are a ragged left-liberal ideology based on four key principles. First, the ideology accepts or is influenced by the mantra that there is no alternative to the market (interventions by states in the wake of Lehman Brothers collapse has not fundamentally changed this). Second, it regards class as an imaginary or outdated concept rather than as a material structural antagonism. Left-liberalism thereby rejects or simply ignores the centrality of labour as a source of capitalist profit. Third, because left-liberalism lacks a dialectical component, new conceptual content is imagined in the void that the ideology helps to create.[3] The world is conceived as multiple points and intersections of power through which information and objects flow.[4] Fourth, the imagined content, which may include notions of risk, cultural intolerance, threat of climate change or corporate power, corruption and venality, become flashpoints for a progressive though ineffectual form of value-rational action.[5] With power appearing diffuse, crimes perpetrated by states, corporations or political leaders are in themselves defused by an ideology that lacks the teeth to cling tenaciously on a single cause. Armies 'of experts, social workers, and so on' are mobilised, Žižek explains, 'to reduce the overall demand (complaint) of a particular group to just this demand, with its particular content' (2000:204).

Concerns about cultural recognition and tolerance of difference fall within the rubric of a cultural-linguistic politics of recognition or what Jameson called a cultural logic. Concerns about the effects of war, poverty and social exclusion on material existence fall within the rubric of a social-material politics of aid and intervention or a social logic. Left-liberalism accentuates both logics recognising capitalism as one of a number of explanations for crises of economy and ecology while rejecting alternative models to capitalism as implausible and undesirable. This 'social-democratic eschatology' exists, in Terry Eagleton's words, 'to repress the past, robbing the class of its hatred by substituting dreams of liberated grandchildren for memories of enslaved ancestors.' (1992:147) Badiou and Žižek develop their respective ideas on the event and act against this post-political background.

Badiou's (2005) politics centres on the notion of the 'event', which he defines as the subtraction of an element within a given situation that has no recognisable place in it. This element constitutes a universal point of exception. A simple example is abstract labour, the combined power of concrete labour exploited for the purposes of surplus profit. The 'proletariat' is the vital element of capitalism but never counted as belonging in it in the sense of having self-determination over its labours as the capitalist has over theirs. Were that to happen the social relations that enable one class to exploit the other would collapse. So if the proletariat were to withdraw or subtract its labour, its presence would be immediately known and it would be in a position to force its own truth or language to create a new universality based on equality and justice. Einstein's theory of relativity counts as an event in science, subtracting from Newtonian physics as the former truth of the situation or 'world' (Badiou 2009). Because there is no language of relativity in Newtonian physics, the event of Einstein effectively re-writes history, forever transforming the world. Likewise, a political event also re-writes history and because it cannot be described in former language the event itself cannot be defined in advance of its taking place. With Žižek, the 'act' exceeds the symbolic coordinates of the order of ethics and establishes from the position of a future-anterior the possibility of politics in the present. The phrase 'politics of the impossible' captures this point, constituting a refusal to accept the post-political limits prescribed by the false universality of liberal-parliamentary democracies. For Badiou and Žižek, then, these disruptive moments bring into existence a subject who stands for the universal dimension of the exception. In the meantime, until an event or act happens, any content we create in the here and now serve as ideological placeholders for establishing common points of opposition. Against the grain of political cynicism, Badiou and Žižek's respective ways of thinking through contemporary ethics leaves open the possibility for revolutionary transformations.

When the ideological accent is on culture, ethics centres on the use of language which makes actions such as the US military ban on pilots putting sexist, racist and homophobic graffiti on the bombs about to be dropped on women, Arabs and homosexuals seem progressive.[6] When the ideological accent is on the social logic, ethics centres on the material effects of material deprivations on life. Jameson's critique of the commodification and celebration of cultural forms, identities and differences still holds, but the emphasis has changed to the extent that ideological legitimation extends to the underside of culture, into the deep recesses of exploitation and corporate venality characterising the ideology of end-capitalism defined in Chapter 2. The ideological accent of the social logic is still cultural in the sense that it remains at the level of material-linguistic indeterminacy and, of course, if the real is the exception of language, then culture-as-language frames our reality. In this sense, the social logic can be thought of as a form of aesthetic production.

Aestheticising the social logic

Adorno (2001:99) made an important distinction between commodification as the indirect outcome of artistic production and the 'direct and undisguised primacy of a precisely and thoroughly calculated efficacy' of an art produced as a commodity. In postmodern theory art is 'intertextual', referencing different artefacts or media and open to divergent subjective readings, but, as Jameson (1993) notes, intertextuality is already calculated into the product. Postmodernism embraced the idea that we are all experts of our own subjective intuitions about the value of art.

Against postmodern relativism, Alain Badiou situates art in its 'truth-moment'. By this he means an art that redefines what is understood by the term. Picasso's *Les Demoiselles d'Avignon* would be an example of the kind of event in art that Badiou is thinking of. The piece was instrumental in redefining and opening up a new artistic horizon. As with Adorno, Badiou (2002, 2007) contrasts art from commodity production and the formulaic repetitions of and references to former works in cultural artefacts designed for mass consumption. The vitality of artistic production lies in an 'exercise of fidelity' with the Idea rather than formula of the original creation. Such fidelity involves testing and verifying through an open process of creation the possibilities of the post-evental world of art. This same procedure would also apply to politics and science as described above.

Without a way to distinguish art through the logic of Adorno or Badiou, for example, art's only logical distinction is exchange-value. Recent works such as Damien Hirst's *For the Love of God*, a diamond-encrusted human skull, had a reported £50 million price tag before it went to market. The exchange-value was the main talking point in discussions on the piece. In the cultural logic, then, the worth of art is determined by its exchange-value. The social logic supplements this with measurements of social value, that is, the extent to which the artefact in some vague sense promotes social causes and helps engender social inclusion. This is also the aesthetic dimension of left-liberalism. It delivers to the spectator of suffering a promissory note that our mawkish interests in the plight of others will some day deliver a political solution; when all it really confirms, relating to Adorno and Horkheimer's (1997:139) critique of the culture industry, is 'that the real point will never be reached, that the diner must always be satisfied with the menu.' The real point that is never reached is the overcoming of poverty and 'social exclusion'. Art is the menu upon which poverty and social inclusion is printed.

A case in point is the Arts Council of England. They sponsored a study on art and social inclusion to explore ways that art could meet governmental targets on inclusion. A number of projects were studied. Successful ones were characterised as,

> creating opportunities for people to participate in arts activities – some of these projects had social and personal objectives such as to increase confidence and self-esteem. The opportunities offered were not merely offering 'access' to a cultural experience that was already there but involved participants actively engaging in and creating art.[7]

The objectives were to, 'Develop and test appropriate methodologies for evaluating arts initiatives with aims relating to social exclusion'; to, 'Identify the characteristics of successful initiatives'; and to, 'Identify approaches that do not work and the reasons for this'. The problem is not so much one of creating opportunities for people to engage in art but how projects that have a social inclusion dimension, so defined, justify art and are calculated into its production. By talking up the benefits of art in helping those deemed excluded or underprivileged, artists and galleries had an answer to those questioning its public value. The trickier issue of justifying art on its intrinsic merits could be avoided. 'Brit Art' exemplified the postmodern celebration of the commodity, but the visible sign of the social justification is always present in high profile public art projects.[8,9]

Aestheticised victims are the loved-up vessels into which our imagined social conscience is transferred. In twists of circumstance, a Haitian who fought against US imperialism becomes the nameless victim of a tragic earthquake. The bad victim becomes the good victim and in these resignifications George W. Bush and Bill Clinton can put aside their political differences and mount a joint appeal addressed to the world. 'There is no greater rallying cry for our common humanity', they say, 'than witnessing our neighbours in distress. And, like any good neighbour, we have an obligation and desire to come to their aid.' (Clinton & Bush 2010) Tragedy does indeed turn to farce and politics collapses into post-politics as all of us are called upon to demonstrate our common humanity. When the victim no longer behaves as a helpless individual into which our compassion can pour by fighting its own battle, 'it magically turns all of a sudden into a terrorist/ fundamentalist/drug-trafficking Other', Zizek (2001:60) writes.

The unarmed victims of Saddam Hussein, and soon of the US and UK, could count on people around the world to march on their behalf on 15 February 2003. Such popular acts of solidarity did not extend to those who fought an armed struggle against the occupation once Saddam was defeated. Frank Furedi described the 'Not in My Name' slogan that protesters used as a reflection of the participants' isolation and disengagement. It is a slogan with a left-liberal tag dangling from it and, as Furedi puts it, a diversity of egos celebrated the 'apolitical strategy for avoiding making statements of judgement.' (2006:43) It is a statement of disassociation, a 'count-me-out' and nothing more says Peter Hallward (cited in Alliez, et al. 2010). This form of politics denotes what Jodi Dean (2009) calls a registration effect. The letter is sent without it mattering whether or not it is received. Dean cites as evidence of this the sheer quantity of Internet websites set up to oppose the Iraq invasion and the diminishing numbers of people involved in protests as the occupation got bloodier.

Christopher Lasch questioned the motives of radical groups such as the 1960s' Weathermen who, he noted,

[H]ad so few practical results to show for their sacrifices that we are driven to conclude that they embraced radical politics in the first place not because it promised practical results but because it served as a new mode of self-dramatisation. (1991:83)

The same can be said of anti-war protests. Unlike the post-Seattle movements, there is no confrontational component of the dramatised aesthetic. Protest becomes fat-free with no risks or sacrifices. Claims as to the motives of protesters notwithstanding, we can see how what appears as an anti-imperialist struggle can garner the support of mainstream media, including the right-wing British tabloid the *Daily Mail* which published a map of the protest route for readers to use. The culture industry's promissory note has many uses. Protests become excuses to celebrate the monstrosities they are organised to oppose. 'These days', Alain Badiou writes, '"celebration" is the name for something like a counter-demonstration.' (2007:107)

There is also a problem of indeterminacy in John Holloway's *Crack capitalism* when he identifies ways that individuals make localised differences, venting anger through music, inspiring students through teaching, struggling against the AIDS virus and so on. Dignity is the weapon, according to Holloway, and 'If capital chooses to repress us, to co-opt us, to imitate us ... let it be clear that we lead the dance.' (2010:50) The difficulty is in translating these local provocations into a more unified struggle that is needed to confront the centralised agencies of power. The danger is that we fetishise the micro-struggles and in doing so neglect the macro ones. There are plenty of examples of the former and few of the latter. There is plenty of salt, but no egg to put it on.

Dissent, as Gramsci noted, is an important component of legitimation because tolerance of it signals that a consensus exists through the rational meditations of subjects, and is not therefore a result of coercive practices. But the state of exception invoked by the 'War on Terror' puts the hegemonic power into the territory of the dissenter. Left-liberalism is validated as the hegemonic position, with the Bush regime along with a handful of states and corporations the aberration. Ideology, in this instance, is seen to belong with the people rather than the state. Whatever the truth of our civil liberties, the tolerance of our citizens, the motives of our leaders and the constant provocation of fear to justify violence, left-liberalism is the default consensus of the most crushing of regimes that the left-liberal US president Barack Obama is now the figurehead of. Fear of the other is now masked as compassion for the other. In this dialectic the state serves the same role as it always has, performing as terrorist and freedom fighter, police officer and friend.

In the context of economic crisis there is ample reason for people to define themselves as victim. The problem is one of identity, that is, who the person sees herself as a victim of and by what accounts she defines herself as a victim. Resistance, for some, is no longer territorial or class based but a struggle of 'singularities' that can break out at every point of the globe. The crisis itself is decentred leaving a vacant centre for any kind of radicalism to fill. While left-liberals criticise the destructive effects of globalised 'deterritorialised' capital, the world continues on its inexorable journey into the economic and ecological abyss. The consensus position confronts the overwhelming material force of capital and disperses itself across a range of issues, anything from opposition to US state-sponsored torture, relief to earthquake victims in Haiti or protests against particular corporations. In the spirit of enterprise, the ethical injunction calls upon everyone to act against the visceral image. The culture of crisis industry turns the image into a global commodity.

Enterprise

Culture of crisis industry

Capital absorbs, transforms and then rebrands critique, turning it into a commodity. Crisis, critique and consumption enter into a virtuous circle. And here, as Georgio Agamben puts it, 'The "imploring eyes" of the Rwandan child, whose photograph is shown to obtain money but who "is now becoming more and more difficult to find alive," may well be the most telling contemporary cipher of the bare life that humanitarian organisations, in perfect symmetry with state power, need.' 1995:133–4) For every crisis there is a victim for NGOs, politicians, celebrities and business to profit from. The mechanism of the culture industry applies here. This was a constellation of forces that worked to provoke and manipulate anxieties for the purpose of selling products with the promise that in purchasing them the constructed lack – of a healthy body, fashionable clothes and so on – would be overcome. Products serve as mirrors for a pseudo-individualised ego. The culture of crisis industry (COCI) operates in the same way. Anxieties are provoked in order to sell products to soothe over the anxieties except here the thing constructed as lacking is not the ideal body shape but rather the ideal conscience. 'Give now', Bill Clinton tells us (cited in Clinton and Bush, 2010), 'and lives will be saved.' There is nothing directly linking a humanitarian crisis that results from an earthquake or crop failure with a Western consumer (although there are clearly socio-economic and political factors that make an earthquake in Haiti that much more destructive than a stronger earthquake in New Zealand). The COCI makes that connection with pleas to our social conscience and in doing so creates a victim whose life hangs by the thread of our charity. We are endowed with the capacity to give life and are morally obliged to do so by our interpellations as the guilty party. We become gods with the capacity to give life as purchasers of the ethical products that charities and businesses advertise.

It is an intoxicating proposition. Taking a look at charities, in 2006 US charitable contributions amounted to $296 billion, 75.6 per cent from individual donors averaging 2 per cent of personal pretax income. In the UK for the financial year 2004–05, the contribution stood at $14.1 billion, or $300 per adult head of the population.[10]

The COCI is a left-liberal-industrial-complex made up of multiple companies, organisations and political parties serving in different ways to turn anxiety into guilt and provide the objects into which guilt can be transferred. The Crisis Industry has its own index for measuring which companies are the most responsive and who the greatest humanitarians are. Covalence's 'ethical quotation system' measures the reputation of companies according to '45 criteria such as labour standards, waste management, product social utility or Human rights policy. It is a barometer of how multinationals are perceived in the ethical field' (Covalence 2010). The top ten 'leaders across sectors' are listed as follows: IBM; Intel Corp; HSBC Holdings; Unilever; Xerox; Cisco Systems; Marks & Spencer; General Electric; Procter & Gamble; and Alcoa Inc. The company's head is featured in the 'Ethisphere' top 100 influential people in business ethics alongside whistleblowers, NGO activists, CEOs such as Mike Duke of Wal-Mart at number six, President of the United States Barack Obama at 33 and Bill Gates at 38 (Ethisphere 2010).

Business performs the role of the subject responding to the desire of the big Other, no longer capital, now the worker as imagined ethical consumer. Like the aberrant George W. Bush, we threaten to castrate business for its misdeeds in Africa, its unwillingness to stock fair trade products and failure to adopt environmental standards. The COCI becomes the champion of our ethical desire and Mike Duke, the president and CEO of Walmart, functions in place of Marx by revealing the secret of the fetishised commodity:

> Customers do want low prices, but not by sacrificing quality. They want products that are more efficient, that last longer and perform better. And increasingly they want information about the entire lifecycle of a product so that they can feel good about buying it. They want to know that the materials in the product are safe ... that it was made well ... and that it was produced in a responsible way. (Walmart 2009)

Through (staged) fear of castration, Walmart learns to speak our language, to desire what we want, and become the ethical equivalent of our ego-ideal. In this carnivalesque moment the slave becomes king day after day, purchase after purchase, empowered as the hegemonic embodiment of a superego authority. We peel away layers of the commodity to discover working practices that threaten our enjoyment of the purchase. Supermarkets go to that place where others are exploited to ensure the product meets the standard criterion for guilt-free enjoyment. Walmart speaks to the little Marxist in all of us by positing itself as guilty, thereby lacking ethical content that it endlessly fills in response to the demands we bombard it with.

Žižek's interpretation of caffeine-free, diet Coca-Cola takes us through this logic. The selling point of the product is its lack of energy and nutrients. The content can never satisfy, it is never enough and so is comparable to *jouissance* – the more you get it the more it is lacking, the guiltier you feel for consuming 'the

Real Thing', the more you want to satisfy a lack. In the case of Walmart, the more it is lacking the more you want it to become more ethical, the guiltier you feel about its lack of ethics when purchasing the products it sells, the more it can do to fulfil this lack and so on. The COCI creates new psychic emollients for the subject to desire by first emptying the fetishised content from its own product and presenting lack-as-content.

Adorno and Horkheimer argued that the more individualised that products are, the more the subjective capacity and need to determine its own identity diminishes – the pseudo-individualised subject recognises herself in a pseudo-individualised product. The iPod in its different iterations with its near infinite variations of content (the tunes) is emblematic of a different kind of pseudo-individualisation. The product is sold to us empty; in an inversion of Adorno and Horkheimer's thesis, it is the subject who pseudo-individualises the product with content that the culture industry makes available to download. Comparable then to the iPod that holds our tunes or the USB storage device that holds our ideas, business corporations act like ethical shells into which the content of a subjective conscience – evoked and manipulated by the COCI – can be transferred. Business is the willing container of our ethical values that are themselves in degrees products of the culture industry.

Ethics has exchange value. Consider Microsoft's Unlimited Potential mission, designed to,

> enable sustained social and economic opportunity for those at the middle and bottom of the world's economic pyramid ... Unlimited Potential aims to [explore] solutions in three key areas: (i) transforming education; (ii) fostering local innovation; and (iii) enabling jobs and opportunities. In these three areas, Microsoft Unlimited Potential can create the greatest possible impact in building a virtuous cycle of sustained social and economic development. Sustainability is a key indicator of effective programs and activities, and is our long-term measure of success. (Microsoft 2010)

The virtuous cycle is of course the circuit of capital. Ethics enters the circuit at multiple points, in the production of knowledge, the distribution of (emotional) affect via the mass production of images of violence and deprivation leading ultimately to exchange and consumption, transforming the use-values of knowledge and their affects into exchange-value.

With so much exposure to images of poverty, war and environmental devastation, there comes a point when we know full well what power does and recognise who the villain really is. In the same way that advertising reveals the mechanism by which it seduces, business reveals the motives behind its ethical pronouncements. We can observe this in Bill Gates' conference speech at the 2008 World Economic Forum, Davos, Switzerland. The 'two great forces of human nature', he declared, are 'self-interest and caring for others':

> Recognition [of capitalism's victims] enhances a company's reputation and appeals to customers. Above all, it attracts good people to an organisation. As such, recognition triggers a market-based reward for good behaviour. In markets where profits are not possible, recognition is a proxy. In markets where profits are possible, recognition can be an added incentive. (cited in World Economic Forum, 2008):

We can read this against the grain of Žižek's critique of Bill Gates as a self-negating capitalist.[11] Gates has fully acknowledged here the underlying instrumental-rational motives guiding his interventions and in doing so self-negates value-rational-action as the reason for his philanthropy. Perhaps the dirty secret of the statement is that Bill Gates really is a socialist and, like all of us who want to transform capitalism, lacks the means to do so individually. Probably not, yet he speaks to both leftists and free-marketeers, placating both ethical consumer and self-interested shareholder. We do the job of ideology by reading into his speeches whatever suits our own desire.

The problem with Bill Gates, like the businesses that brand their products with ethical signifiers, is (as always) that the structural antagonism shaping existence must of course be elided. Capitalist ethics cannot be anything other than new clothes in the above respect because business cannot do anything other than prioritise profit if it is to keep afloat. The COCI, of which Microsoft is a part, is able to colonise left-critique, doing so in recognition that there is a market for ethical products when there is no apparent effective strategy for challenging the system. The COCI compensates for the lack of political options and in its pseudo-ethical products offers the palliative to quiet the nagging sense that something has to be done. And it goes further than this by reminding us of the need to act, stoking anxieties about the future of society and inducing feelings of guilt to create demand for ethical products. It reverses the role that Adorno and Horkheimer assigned to the culture industry. It becomes the lacking agent to whom the subject-as-customer makes a demand. The Industry acquires the language of the ethical subject in response to a barely articulated ethical desire that it can shape and reproduce in a more legible way. It uses the crisis of capitalism as the instrument of seduction. Without reference to actual humanitarian disasters and structural deficiencies, there can be no truth-substance to the ethical driver.

Commodifying crises

The culture of crisis industry is made up of a number of competing organisations representative of what Althusser called the Ideological State Apparatus (ISA), which include corporations, NGOs, political parties and grassroots movements. The connection between ethical stance, action and commodity is sometimes abstract (in the case of companies using surplus profit for an ethical cause) and often indirect (in the case of grassroots movements with no interest in surplus-value). The connection between these agents within a COCI only makes sense as a totality and in that totality we find the multiple disseminated signifiers of crises.

The pseudo-individualisation of a social conscience cannot happen without the help of a signifier around with which to construct the ethical value. Naomi Klein, in a way reminiscent of Harvey's argument that capitalism has returned to a form of primitive smash-and-grab accumulation, examines how business profits from natural and human-made disasters. She calls this a disaster capitalism complex of companies that make substantial profits even as destruction is occurring. The destructions she has in mind include anything from wars of aggression to the collapse of economies and natural disasters, the kind of crises serving as marketing props for the COCI.

Businesses, Klein notes, are contracted to repair the societies that have been destroyed and, moreover, such as in the case of Iraq, to be involved for the duration of the destruction by supplying anything from security personnel to catering services. The underlying logic was explained by Milton Friedman, who she cites as saying that 'only a crisis – actual or perceived – produces real change. When that crisis occurs, the actions that are taken depend on the ideas that are lying around. That, I believe, is our basic function: to develop alternatives to existing policies, to keep them alive and available until the politically impossible becomes politically inevitable.' (Klein 2007:6) A case that Klein refers to is the privatisation of New Orleans schooling immediately after the Hurricane Katrina disaster. Charter schools, publicly funded institutions run by private companies, were built in place of the schools that were damaged and destroyed. Whereas Klein is describing a material intervention by business on the ground of where crises take place, crises serve the COCI as devices to evoke feelings of collective responsibility for the purposes of selling products and services. Whereas in disaster capitalism profits are made on-site, the COCI serves business over a longer duration and in a more indirect way by encouraging the consumer to demand the products and services that have been assigned ethical content. The COCI helps visualise and disseminate through popular media sources the resulting pain and suffering from crises of various magnitudes to expand markets for ethical products and services. It appropriates, evokes and defuses crises.

The COCI appropriates crises, typically ones that are either unanticipated and significant in scale or gaining considerable media attention. Examples include natural disasters such as the 2010 Haiti earthquake, unanticipated terrorist acts such as '9/11' and sudden economic crises. Events of this kind require an immediate response from states, organisations, private companies and the general public.

Let us consider the Haiti earthquake. The country was in crisis long before 2010, but it is the earthquake that frames a separate story to the one that could be told about the liberation struggles against slavery, imperialism and occupation.[12] Being the most impoverished country in the hemisphere helps in providing a suitable backdrop for turning an earthquake disaster into a mass media event for Bush and Clinton to get involved in. The tissue manufacturer Kimberly-Clark, as 'a leading corporate partner of the American Red Cross Annual Disaster Giving Program (ADGP)' responded to Bush and Clinton's (2010) plea for 'food, water, shelter, and first aid supplies' by designating 'a portion of [its financial] gift' to the fund for earthquake relief, assembling 'a significant donation of much-needed Kimberly-Clark health care products, diapers, feminine care and tissue products from … [its] … local operations in the Dominican Republic' (Kimberly-Clark 2010). The non-governmental, entertainment, retail and newspaper left-liberal industrial complex joined this effort by repackaging, reissuing, promoting and selling the nauseating 'Everybody Hurts' by REM as 'Helping Haiti – Everybody Hurts'. The Amazon website described the product as follows (2010):

> The single will split all proceeds 50/50 between DEC (Disasters Emergency Committee) and The Sun newspaper's 'Helping Haiti' appeal. Prime Minister Gordon Brown has pledged to waive VAT on the single. Not less than £1 from the sale of this CD and 100% of any profits Amazon makes from this single will be divided equally between Disasters Emergency Committee (registered charity no 1062638) and The Sun's 'Helping Haiti' Fund. Monies paid to The Sun's Helping Haiti Fund will be paid directly to a charitable trust set up for The Sun by the Charities Aid Foundation (registered charity number 268369), and all monies received by that trust will be paid to registered charities to help those affected by the earthquake in Haiti.

Each 'contribution' or 'gift', as Kimberley-Clark calls it, adds symbolic value to the raw object – earthquake in this instance – and enhances the profile of the donator. When two adversaries such as Bush and Clinton put aside their differences to make a joint appeal we know we are witnessing an earthquake disaster on an unprecedented scale. When Murdoch's *The Sun* newspaper, Gordon Brown, the taxpayer, the pop band REM and Amazon get involved, they demonstrate the ethical value of their enterprising skills by providing a service to be enjoyed on behalf of the victim.

The ecological crisis is pumped up with such promotions, keeping alive the prospect for the creation of value for a newly created mass market for ethical products. All of us and none of us are responsible. The events are depoliticised while also commercialised. The economic crisis works accordingly, and products to satisfy demand in response to it come on-stream. Barack Obama's inauguration speech prepares the ground,

> So let us summon a new spirit of patriotism; of service and responsibility where each of us resolves to pitch in and work harder and look after not only ourselves, but each other. Let us remember that if this financial crisis taught us anything, it's that we cannot have a thriving Wall Street while Main Street suffers – in this country, we rise or fall as one nation; as one people. (cited in BBC News 2008)

Where crises threaten business interests, the COCI can help defuse them politically. By marking everyone as victim of and solution to the problem of capitalism, the material fact of political economy is confronted in diffuse ways without the ideology being compromised. In this mix enters the banker, consumer, property owner and politician each commanded to atone for their guilt by acting in a more responsible way. In the Haiti example, the crisis is localised and can therefore be commodified in name. The sign 'Haiti earthquake disaster' is consumable, not 'the crises tendencies of the capitalist mode of production' which is unlikely to become a brand anytime soon. But 'the debt crisis', 'the housing crisis' and 'the unemployment crisis' can help bring into existence films, TV shows, services and government and corporate 'initiatives' that respond to new anxieties developing around them.

There are well-documented cases of the media amplifying social issues, creating moral panics, manufacturing fear and shaping political discourses. The COCI amplifies social issues, creates panics, manufactures fear and shapes political discourses for business to trade on. The whole industry can get involved in the case of a large media-event such as Haiti. There are also minor crises either in terms of their scale or media interest that the COCI feeds off. A case in point is Starbucks (2010) support for clean water with their Ethos Water brand, which the company describes as a 'brand with a social mission' to 'help children around the world get clean water'. The 'bottom line' is that 'putting people before products just makes good common sense.' Starbucks (2010) presents itself as 'pro-active' rather than 're-active', 'to inspire and nurture the human spirit – one person, one cup, and one neighbourhood at a time.'

As argued in Chapter 3, the individual strives to become human in the image of business but also by being ethical in response to the broader demands of the COCI, and in preparation for employers that recognise the contribution an ethical actor brings to a firm. Crises are manufactured for the purposes of presenting the object as somehow emblematic of what it means to be human. The COCI can be called upon to help with a 'humanitarian' crisis and also help justify state intervention in certain 'troublespots' of the world. This relationship was highlighted by the Secretary of State, under George W. Bush, Colin Powell, when talking about the invasion of Afghanistan. 'NGOs', he said, 'are such a force multiplier for us, such an important part of our combat team... [We are] all committed to the same, singular purpose to help humankind...' (cited in Douzinas 2007:61). Arundhati Roy puts it another way, that NGOs 'end up functioning like the whistle on a pressure cooker. They divert and sublimate political rage, and make sure that it does not build to a head.' (cited in Davis 2006:79)

There is always the danger, of course, that such a wealth of issues demanding our services creates a condition of apathy. As Adorno reminds us,

Indiscriminate kindness towards all carries the constant threat of indifference and remoteness to each, attitudes communicated in their turn to the whole. Injustice is the medium of true justice. Unrestricted benevolence becomes affirmation of all the bad that exists, in that it minimises its difference from the traces of good and levels it to that generality which prompts the hopeless conclusion of bourgeois-mephistophelian wisdom, that all that sees the light of day deserves to go the selfsame way. (2000:77)

Apathy denotes indifference. The size of the COCI industry suggests anything but indifference, the question is what are we acting for, perhaps simply to preserve the image of concern through the constant pressure to engage in ritualistic gestures of social responsibility.

The COCI defuses political crises, such as when protest movements force an issue onto the political agenda. One example, already touched upon, is the appropriation of 'artistic' demands of student protesters in May 1968 by organisations, to create what Boltanski and Chiapello call a *new spirit of capitalism*. A more recent and well-documented example is the co-option by business and NGOs of the anti-capitalist movement. In 2005, six years after the WTO protests in Seattle, the G8 met in St Andrews and 'anti-globalisation' protesters converged in Edinburgh to demonstrate for a resolution on global poverty with the full support of NGOs and the mass media. Sir Bob Geldof became the self-nominated spokesman overshadowing the demonstration by announcing a follow-up to the 1985 Live Aid jamboree. The BBC's entertainment website waxed lyrical about the event when it took place,

> A TV audience of several hundred million were watching the gigs, ahead of the G8 summit of leaders next week ... Almost all the singers involved took the opportunity to explain their reasons for performing. Taking to the stage Madonna asked the crowd: 'Are you ready to start a revolution? Are you ready to change history? I said, are you ready?' ... More than 26.4 million people from around the world sent text messages on Saturday in support of the Live 8 campaign to cancel the debts of the poorest countries, setting a world record, organisers said. (BBC News 2005b)

Geldof's role in defusing the effect of the demonstration was illustrated in the More4 (UK television channel) documentary *Starsuckers* (Hilary 2010). 'Make Poverty History', the slogan of the 2005 demonstration, was a love note delivered to the self. Whereas the war could hypothetically be stopped without contradicting the interests of capital, the 'Make Poverty History' slogan was a plea to those in charge to deliver the impossible. It asked those who in other circumstances would be held accountable for poverty to do the job of reducing poverty for us, this time proudly in our name. The anti-capitalist movement was now co-opted into the mechanism of the COCI helping in the expansion of the market for ethical products NGOs are able to supply.

The safety drills on passenger aircraft provide a useful analogy to summarise the post-politics of the COCI appeal. As procedures for surviving a plane crash are talked through, we are reminded of just how vulnerable we are should a plane malfunction. The event of a crash would be catastrophic to human life, but there is a lifejacket under the seat should we happen to land safely on water. The problem is maximal and the solution is minimal, reminding us of how vulnerable we are while offering a modicum of reassurance. The other is a novel victim of an earthquake or IMF structural-adjustment policy, the inferior or one-dimensional 'I'. In their 'dark skins and incomprehensible language', their 'colourful and lazy lives', in their 'suffering and perseverance', Costas Douzinas writes, 'we see the beautiful people we are' (2007:85). In a sleight of hand, the oppressor, the exploiter and the affluent middle classes become heroes providing the life jackets for distribution. We bear witness to destruction and the bourgeois in turn call upon us to act, not for justice but to have determination over the image of action, to wrest a piece of *jouissance* from those fighting on the ground by signifying their cause for our enjoyment. Passivity is the instrument of guilt fetishism.

Enjoyment

Guilt fetishism

We arrive at the point in this chapter where the various arguments can be brought together and linked with an element only brushed upon so far, the enjoying mode of left-liberal ethics, and bring forth the concept of guilt fetishism. Freud wrote a short essay on fetishism primarily about a man whose arousal was obtained from the shine on a woman's nose. Freud interpreted the shine as a substitute for the man's inability to come to terms with the fact that women have no penis. There is a dual aspect to this, however, in an affirmation and denial of castration. The fetish signals both the acknowledgement of and vulnerability to castration (symbolically referring to a loss of power rather than a literal penis) and a denial of and triumph over castration through the discovery of a lost object, the shine on the nose in this case. Money has a similar appeal in becoming the fetishised object of exchange arousing a desire for enterprise. The commodity fetishist ascribes to money value that it does not intrinsically possess (a penis) as a way to come to terms with the social relations it denies (castration). In Freud's example, the fetish is surplus to normal psychosexual behaviour. With commodity fetishism, money is a normalised surplus. In other words, the fetish is the condition by which money obtains symbolic value for capital to circulate and is not generally regarded a perverse fixation. Guilt fetishism relates to fetishism in both a Freudian and Marxist sense.[13]

Christopher Lasch cites Erich Fromm, who argued that feminism, Marxism and psychoanalysis have converged to form a 'patricentric' personality. It is a person who 'experiences suffering as guilt instead of injustice, accepts his lot instead of trying to change the social conditions that make him unhappy, and "identifies with the aggressor" instead of attempting to unite the victims of aggression against the prevailing social system.' (1984:228) The COCI seeks to generalise this phenomenon. The object the guilt fetishist gets off on is every failed attempt to satisfy a desire to rid itself of the image of suffering, enjoying the repeated failures to take political action.

First, guilt fetishism is an excessive fixation on an image of a person suffering castration/lack of food, shelter, basic civil liberties and so on. These objects serve as empty vessels into which guilt can be transferred every time we make a donation. Campbell Jones (2010) makes this point about transference in his essay on recycling. Everyone is called upon to recycle and so no one in particular is held to account for ecological destruction. Recycling is a means by which we transfer or get rid of our guilt. As Žižek writes,

> By surrendering my innermost content, including my dreams and anxieties, to the Other, a space opens up in which I am free to breathe: when the Other laughs for me, I am free to take a rest; when the Other is sacrificed instead of me, I am free to go on living with the awareness that I did atone for my guilt, and so on. (1997:109)

This corresponds to a general term Žižek refers to as 'interpassivity'. The thing enjoys on our behalf, the audience on television shows laugh for us and the people of the Bolivarian Republic of Venezuela enact socialism for us. The Other also enjoys poverty for us. An example of this transference is found in the advertising campaign of the Fairtrade brand, Divine chocolate. One of its campaign posters had a picture of a healthy looking black woman seductively holding a piece of chocolate while standing in front of a clichéd image of what appears like an African village. The slogan read, 'Eat Poverty History'. Divine commands us to enjoy a product that is unhealthy for the body and sourced from countries where labour is highly exploited. The superego injunction is signified in the imperative form of the verb to eat. The thing we are told to eat is poverty, and the promise is that if we eat enough of it we can satisfy our hunger. We Make discomfort about the Poverty of our politics History by consuming chocolate as a cause of poverty, and thus transfer our guilt from the chocolate product we consume to the person who the chocolate signifies. The nasty substance contained in the chocolate – not sugar but exploitation – is processed out so that we can eat chocolate without feeling guilty. Capitalism has an endless supply of poverty for us to consume, with the COCI ensuring that demand is kept high with its images of poverty and the healthy consequences of our ethical consumption. We never get enough chocolate because third-world hunger is never conquered, guilt is never gotten rid of and hence we return to the same point of being hungry for chocolate all over again. As with another of Divine's slogans, we are always 'Hungry to change the world'. The COCI satisfies a hunger for ethical products and through Divine the absolute poverty of our politics is sutured.

According to Jacques Ranciere the 'intolerable image' of suffering can serve a political function by inducing people to take action. But the intolerable image can also induce commercial activity. The political ambiguity of the intolerable image should here be noted when he writes that,

> The spectator ... must be convinced that she is herself guilty of sharing in the prosperity rooted in imperialist exploitation of the world. And she must further feel guilty about being there and doing nothing; about viewing these images of pain and death, rather than struggling against the powers responsible for it. In short, she must already be feeling guilty about viewing the image that is to create the feeling of guilt. (Ranciere 2009:85)

The Gift Aid scheme removes the spectacle. The scheme was set up by the UK government to allow people to contribute a small part of their taxation to charities, which then claim back from the government a basic rate of tax (HM Revenue & Customs 2010). The online trading website eBay (2010) explains how this form of giving need not cost anything to the consumer:

> In the spirit of giving, eBay rewards your generosity by offering the eBay for Charity Fee Credit Policy. When you create a listing with eBay for Charity and that item sells, eBay will credit the basic Insertion and Final Value Fees back to you, equal to the percentage of the final sale price that you choose to donate.

It is the thought that counts, after all. By automating giving, the whole process is rationalised to allow the consumer to enjoy guilt-free without the image of suffering having to be seen: in mind and out of sight.

Like a starstruck fan, Bill Gates in his 2008 speech at Davos talked about an encounter with the pop star Bono:

> A few years ago I was sitting in a bar here in Davos with Bono. Late at night, after a few drinks, he was on fire, talking about how we could get a percentage of each purchase from civic-minded companies to help change the world. He kept calling people, waking them up, and handing me the phone to show me the interest. Well, it's taken time to get this going, but he was right. If you give people a chance to associate themselves with a

cause they care about, while buying a great product, they will. (World
Economic Forum 2008)

Product (RED) was the outcome.[14] A number of companies
including Apple, Gap, Converse, Dell, Starbucks and Nike are
signed up to the campaign. Each company donates up to 50 per
cent of its profit from (RED) branded products – a red iPod, a
red tee-shirt and so on. This is then used 'to buy and distribute
antiretroviral medicine to our brothers and sisters dying of AIDS
in Africa' ([RED] 2010); in short: '[b]uy (RED), saves lives. [sic.]
It's as simple as that.' Gap shows us how to gift our guilt in five
easy steps (quoted from their website):

1. A shopper notes that the Gap (PRODUCT)[RED] apparel cost
   the same as other Gap apparel.
2. Shopper buys the Gap (PRODUCT)[RED] apparel. Gap sends a
   contribution of 50% of profits directly to The Global Fund –
   not to (RED).
3. The Global Fund uses 100% of this money to finance HIV
   health and community support programs in Africa, with a
   focus on women and children.
4. The contribution helps a person affected by HIV.
5. Shopper has some new Gap (PRODUCT)[RED] clothes and
   helped save a person's life. And, they can continue to help
   when they choose (RED) the next time they shop or they can
   get INSPI(RED) to donate more money directly to the Global
   Fund.

The second step anticipates a cynical response to the motives while
the third informs us that the proceeds go towards helping the
ubervictims, those such as woman and children whose images can
easily be appropriated to present a sense of the other's vulnerability
and helplessness. By the fifth stage everyone is a winner. The
consumer has a new tee-shirt to enjoy guilt-free. The new clothes
act as a disguise for the emptiness of such gestures, branding the
self as a conscientious consumer to remind others of their responsibility for AIDS victims. Gap adds the left-liberal aesthetic to its

brand and, as Foucault would have noted, the purchaser of the tee-shirt polices other people's ethics at a micro-level by reminding them to act ethically too.

Another example, not linked to Product (RED), but rich with symbolic potency is MAC cosmetics' *Viva Glam* lipstick. The profits on the sale of specific shades again go to help HIV/AIDS victims.[15] The pop stars Cyndi Lauper and 'the electric Lady Gaga!' are called upon to market the product by plumping up their lips with it. We can be Lady Gaga and Bill Gates all in one by staining our lips with (RED) signifiers of HIV/AIDS. Lauper and Gaga are perfect role models,

> A singer/songwriter, Lauper characteristically uses her fame as a performer to help make her message heard. Whether touring the country to assist food banks or helming the True Colors Fund, which lobbies for GLBT [gay, lesbian, bisexual and transgender] equality, Lauper stands for what she believes in and, when it comes to HIV/AIDS, that's safe sex. With the launch of VIVA GLAM Cyndi, she looks forward to helping support women who have contracted HIV/AIDS through rape. (MAC 2010)

As for Gaga,

> A legend in her own time whose shock value now comes with a couture tag, she jokes about 'changing the world one sequin at a time.' With the launch of VIVA GLAM Gaga, that could be one shade at a time. Her take on HIV/AIDS prevention: be selective about those you love. (MAC 2010)

The superego has permitted us to enjoy. It provides the additional substance, the alibi, to go on living in a manner we are used to. As a bonus we can feel good in the knowledge that despite the visible strains of poverty and exploitation around the world, the stains on our lips will visibly show that we have done our bit to atone for our guilt. The ethical subject wears capitalism's new clothes and MAC's new *Viva Glam Gaga* lipstick.

While a particular famine is yesterday's news, poverty and, for the foreseeable future, HIV/AIDS are all our yesterdays, todays and tomorrows. Poverty is a master signifier, alongside climate change, of the many minor crises such as earthquakes that strike impoverished regions of the world. Poverty is close to the most intimate of zones. The signifier brushes up to the real cause, never quite connecting with it, offering a constant supply of products to keep the obvious truth buried on eBay. With the poverty version of 'Everybody Hurts', blood is wrapped in cellophane, stained on the lips of every willing consumer. To enjoy the representation, something of the Real has to be seen. Marcuse, again from his essay on tolerance, is useful here:

> All points of view can be heard: the Communist and the Fascist, the Left and the Right, the white and the Negro, the crusaders for armament and for disarmament. Moreover, in endlessly dragging debates over the media, the stupid opinion is treated with the same respect as the intelligent one, the misinformed may talk as long as the informed, and propaganda rides along with education, truth with falsehood. (Cited in Wolff, et al. 1969:108)

It is not that truth lies in falsehood but, as Marcuse explains, truth sits alongside falsehood, and this way critique breaks against the multiple balustrades of hurt. We can think of the sheer nylon covering a woman's legs as an analogy for this materialist indeterminacy. The fetishistic appeal of hosiery relates to what Freud has said about the girdle covering the 'castrated' part of the woman's body (cited in Phillips 2006). The 'thing' is imagined in the place that the material covers. The significance of nylon is that we get to sneak a peak at the bare flesh underneath without getting too close to the thing. The gauze nylon material functions like the half closed fingers children place in front of their eyes to protect themselves from seeing something they secretly take delight in. Flesh appears in micro sections between the nylon fabric creating a see-through effect, a pseudo-affective and intellectual encounter with the critical substance. This way the untouchable flesh is enjoyed at a safe distance with the material smoothing out blemishes and creating the illusion of a deterritorialised surface all the way down the legs. The gap of inconsistency between ideology and reality is sutured by the thinnest of fabrications. The shinier the fabric the more it catches our gaze, the more we feel guilty for taking pleasure in such a thing. The COCI nylon-izes or fetishises reality for our pleasure. We can see just how thin the material is when we again call upon Walmart's Mike Duke to tell us about his 'big picture view',

> Despite all the work that's been done, we see only bits of information, but not the full picture across the supply chain. We don't know the patterns, hidden costs and impacts of the products we make and sell. Nor do we have a single source of data or a common standard for evaluating the sustainability of products.
>
> If we want to help the customer of the future live better, we need that data. We need that big picture view. (Cited in Walmart 2009)

The phrase 'big picture view' exemplifies the ideological premise of the COCI. The big picture view is the image of the big Other as the big Other would like us to see it, as possessing a social conscience and thereby revealing the chain of social relations otherwise obscured by the fetishisation of money. Commodity fetishism is defetishised in the manner of the nylon: the shinier the ideology, the thinner the fabric, the smoother and more apparent the underlying substance. We are in touching distance of the nakedness the little boy is yet to pronounce.

Another example is Amnesty International's (2010) 'throw a party for human rights' fund raising and awareness campaign. Disturbing images and narratives about torture and oppression encourage the subject to work to displace the image from its conscience. At a 'human rights party' the images of incarceration and torture are held at a safe distance, there for us to dance around and enjoy. The event permits us to have fun while affording us the opportunity to gift our guilt in the form of a donation to those we party for. There is a release of tension as each step on the dance floor transfers guilt to the victim enjoying suffering for the pleasure of the dancers. The nylon sheath is shinier, the 'party' polishes the tortured bodies to catch our gaze and command our coins without disrupting the proximal dance. In every instance guilt is transferred from consumer to whoever is signified as lacking food, shelter, human rights and so on. Guilt is fetishised as the 'universal vanishing mediator' between anxiety and object that signifies lack of this kind.

There is an important difference between Freud's fetishist and the guilt fetishist. Freud claimed that the fetishist saw their proclivity as advantageous because it provided them with a source of pleasure that other men lacked. In the case of the guilt fetishist, the pleasure is disavowed in the first place – we cannot accept that poverty is something we enjoy – yet, unlike the man who took pleasure in the shine on women's noses, the object of the guilt fetishist is as general and banal as men's fascination with nylon hosiery. Disclosing the pleasure one derives from another's suffering, were it recognised in the first place, would entirely negate the transference mechanism by marking the person as a perverted sadist.

Another of Divine's slogans, 'Not so guilty pleasure', illustrates the point. The slogan implies that a residue of guilt remains after the product has been consumed, causing the consumer to want more. Without a relationship to guilt, the product contains no message beyond its function to literally fill hunger. To disclose the underlying mechanism, Divine would need to produce a slogan such as 'Enjoy Poverty', the one the artist Renzo Martens uses to highlight the way charities commodify poverty in Africa.

It is only when I exchange my guilt by passing it on to another, perhaps when buying a phosphate-free detergent brand, that my ethical credentials are realised. If revolution was the object for getting rid of guilt its realisation would leave us effectively broke. The object cannot deliver but the more it appears to be delivering the greater the ethical value. The transcendence of capitalism serves as an object cause of desire, with every identifiable desire to support an ethical cause operating as its symbolic substitute. The labours of CEOs, politicians, celebrities and volunteers add value to the particular crisis, profit from which is realised when guilt is exchanged. As with any product, there is a risk of overaccumulation.

A significant amount of labour is embodied in the production of the commodity form of 'Haiti earthquake disaster', the aid workers, celebrities, politicians, business leaders, charity adminis-trators, fund raisers and so on. The weight of guilt is heavy at first. There is a strong compulsion to help out and the social reward for doing so is high. Despite the ongoing problems in Haiti, eventually the market is saturated with earthquake related products, feelings of responsibility diminish as profits decline affecting the amount of labour invested in it. Another crisis is required, a new famine or earthquake.

The signifier of crisis accumulates value as it passes between agencies each impregnating the code, adding symbolic value to it. The labour invested in the sign helps in its valorisation, contributing to the profit the object makes: in the case of charities, donations over and above the cost of running the organisation. The power of the sign of crisis reaches a saturation point for a number of reasons. Demand slackens when the crisis subsides and there are no new ones being reproduced that are shiny enough to catch our gaze. Or, the market is saturated with too many products, either relating to the same issue, or many different ones causing us to feel overwhelmed. The fortunes of NGOs depend on a constant supply of new and novel crises. Oxfam, Greenpeace and others not only compete with one another, they also have to ensure that the product they specialise in does not go out of fashion. This is easier for NGOs whose raw staples are always in supply, poverty and ecological disasters for example. Corporations, however, are more flexible because they do not primarily exist as charitable organisations so they can diversify their product by chopping and changing between causes without diluting the brand.

The ethical brand can also be damaged when there are a number of competing, contradictory and confusing messages about the causes of crises. The climate change industry suffers from competing claims about the effect of industrial production and consumption on the ecosystem. BP, which invested heavily in its environmental brand, contributes to the COCI but saw the value of its contribution undermined by the Deepwater disaster (see Chapter 6). There are the same crises tendencies in the fortunes of NGOs, their organisations being dependent on publicity designed to sustain the emotive force of crises and segue these new signs of crises into a convincing narrative.

The superego punishes us for not making empty pronouncements and handing over a few coins when under pressure to
support different causes. We feel obliged to comply when
supermarkets allow charity workers to fill our bags to raise money
for Children in Need. We are under pressure to buy the Fairtrade
brand knowing full well that the effects of our actions are likely
to be minimal, if having any effect at all. In every instance guilt
is transferred from consumer to whoever is signified as lacking.
Guilt is fetishised as the universal vanishing mediator between
anxiety and object that signifies lack. There is no alternative,
we might as well consume 'ethically' and sometimes this is the
only course of action open to us. Such gestures may signify that
some of us do care and feel helpless to do anything more than
consume Fairtrade coffee. Whatever our motives, there can be no
satisfaction from such gestures or claim to ethical responsibility.

Conclusion

The chapter charted a path from politics of difference through to
what has been described as the indeterminate, non-dialectical and
deterritorialised social logic signifying material deprivation. In this
mix we find a leftist critique of capitalism and a liberalistic agenda
that business, politicians, NGOs and cultural industries can easily
appropriate and hegemonise. Capitalism has entered a crisis phase
at the level of representation, transforming politics into a series of
visibly reproducible and unfolding tragedies, disasters, struggles
and injustices embodied in the helpless plight of the other suffering
poverty. Mega-crises of the global economy and ecology, with a
visual coating of poverty, feed into the narrative significations
of end-capitalism for the purposes of profit. The engine of these
significations is the culture of crisis industry, which provokes
and manipulates anxieties to generate and generalise feelings of
responsibility for the other's wellbeing. We are all held responsible
for the survival of others, all guilty and all in need of products
and services we can offload our guilt onto.

The ethical imperative is characterised by the need to recognise
and preserve cultural difference, the responsibility of state and

individual to insure against the destructive impact of markets and an 'all hands on decks' call to steer the boat through choppy waters towards a calmer sea of socially embedded free-markets somewhere over the horizon. From the postmodern emphasis on cultural difference through to non-dialectical critiques of the market, the ideology has served to quilt, or gather together, the floating signifiers of rage and injustice into a kaleidoscopic pattern of an infinite superficiality disconnecting the Real of political economy as the colours circulate before our implacable and yet satiated gaze. The culture of crisis industry makes good use of this material. It markets the material lack in the other. It signifies anxiety as a disavowed guilt for another's suffering, generalised de-class-ified responsibility for the ills of the world. The other becomes a vessel for the ethical content, hitherto identified as belonging to the subject, to transfer over to the commodified object as the pseudo-individualised quantum of politics proper. Like any hegemonic ideology, left-liberalism is accompanied by a level of dissent. Whether or not the Bush regime, its supporters and allies, counted as dissenters depends on how far we want to take this argument. One thing is clear, however, without any determinate cause for the left to identify and act upon we leave the field wide open for the Right to do precisely this with its politics of fear and hatred. Guilt can easily lead to resentment.

Deleuze and Guattari (1987), who distinguish between what they call movements of interest and movements of flight, can be deployed to examine the political potential of any group or organisation that calls upon our services. Movements of interest are concerned with preserving the privileged position to which they belong. A movement of flight subtracts itself from the situation by exceeding it. The struggles of May 1968 are an example of movements of flight. Deleuze and Guattari are also keen to stress that when movements assume a particular identity they are easily appropriated into the capitalist 'axiomatic' – trade unions, the women's movement and NGOs being examples of this. Movements can be judged according to whether they are *virtual*, as in engaged in an open process of struggle – a virtue of becoming – or *actual*, as in crystallised around particular institutionalised interests. For a time, the post-Seattle movements were arguably virtual or at least had the potential of combining as a revolutionary force. In its initial phase, the anti-war movement could have developed into something that really threatened the imperialist powers operating in Iraq. Movements that belong to the left-liberal complex are those designed for and/or co-opted into the COCI and, as such, are movements of interest.

It is easy in end-capitalism to fall into the pit of 'enlightened false consciousness.' There is nothing naïve about taking part in struggles that have the potential of doing more than add 'a little walnut oil in the wheels, crumbs of holy wafer for the disinherited' (Badiou 2008:102). However, we need theory to distinguish activity from pseudo-activity. It is worth reminding ourselves of what Adorno said at the beginning of *Negative Dialectics*, that 'Philosophy, which once seemed obsolete, lives on because the moment to realise it was missed.' (2007:3) It also lives on as a way to discern the limits and potentialities of left-oriented movements and organisations.

If the possibilities for victories on different magnitudes are open, it is better sometimes to be involved in those movements than not participating in any struggles at all. Nevertheless, to simply do something rather than nothing is no compensation for the horrors capitalism unleashes and for this reason we need local struggles to acquire a universal dimension.

5

NAKED ENJOYMENT

When Steve Jobs, the CEO of Apple Corps, launched the mark 4 iPhone, he confirmed what Adorno and Horkheimer, Vance Packard and many others have said about consumer products: they sell because of how they make us feel, not because of what they do. This is how he pitched the product:

> Now, this is really hot ... you got to see this thing in person, it's one of the most beautiful designs you've ever seen ... Glass on the front and rear, stainless steel running around ... its closest kin is like a beautiful old Leica camera.

We can almost see the audience salivating as Jobs speaks. The 'i' is that magical symbol, the dollar sign of excess marking the thing out as special. And in many respects it is a cut above the rest, possessing that little extra 'it' that gets us excited. We thrive on it, and Apple and videogame companies such as Nintendo, with its own brand of i-products (Wii, DSi), supply us with it. The consumer, though, is no longer innocent. She is asked to be ethical in her choice of products and, since the financial crisis, restrained in her desires for them. But a world without excess, a world in which everything merely functions, would be stripped of everything essential to human life. Excess is not the issue, rather the form it takes and how those essential superfluities of fun, play and enjoyment are increasingly enclosed in, and have nowhere to go except, the clamshell designs of consumer products and the open plan offices of fun companies. Adorno was not an enemy of play, or a killjoy of fun. He wrote in *Minima Moralia* that,

> In his purposeless activity the child, by a subterfuge, sides with use-value against exchange value. Just because he deprives the things with which

he plays of their mediated usefulness, he seeks to rescue in them what is benign towards men and things. The little trucks travel nowhere and the tiny barrels on them are empty; yet they remain true to their destiny by not performing, not participating in the process of abstraction that levels down that destiny, but instead abides as allegories of what they are specifically for ... The unreality of games gives notice that reality is not yet real. (Adorno 2000:228)

'The "struggle for existence"', Marcuse wrote, 'is originally a struggle for pleasure, culture begins with the collective implementation of this aim.' (2006:125) But in capitalism, the institutions of the reality principle – the school, prison, workplace – dominate and transform the erotic base of culture. One could be forgiven, though, when flicking through television channels, picking up a magazine or surfing the net, for thinking that Marcuse's dream has been realised. Pleasure is everywhere, porn is in our eyes, the possibilities of play are endless and in such a world there is no excuse not to have a good time. Pleasure is exhausting. Pleasure is a duty, writes Pierre Bourdieu:

Thus, whereas the old morality of duty, based on the opposition between pleasure and good, induces a generalised suspicion of the 'charming and attractive', a fear of pleasure and a relation to the body made up of 'reserve', 'modesty' and 'restraint', and associates every satisfaction of the forbidden impulses with guilt, the new ethical avant-garde urges a morality of pleasure as duty. This doctrine makes it a failure, a threat to self-esteem, not to 'have fun' ... pleasure is not only permitted but demanded, on ethical as much as on scientific grounds. (2003:367)

Johan Huizinga described 'man' as a player or *homo ludens*, observing that free activity has its own space and time, the playground and playtime in common parlance. Like the little boy playing with his trucks, play for Huizinga is pre-subjective, non-commodified and therefore non-instrumentalised. Gadamer (cited in Sutton-Smith 1997:182) calls play a transformative experience at the locus of subjectivity, 'an experience changing the person who experiences it'. Play is not a chaotic or even disorderly activity. There are rules to games and in every playful act there are unspoken codes without which play would be a mess of human drives and desires. But then, with its rules, and its spaces and times, play can also be rationalised; play can be regulated and commodified, its nature transformed and appropriated for the purposes of surplus-value. In short, play is turned into an alien object that can only be accessed through work and bought in commodified consumption.

Our ability to transform nature in our own image has no equivalent in the animal world. Play, however, is something animals also do. Also unique to humans, though, is the potential for play to become an object that stands opposed to her. This chapter is about the alienation of play, forced fun and the injunctions to enjoy. It is about the fun ethic and play as objects turned against the self. The commodity is at the heart of naked enjoyment.

Enjoyment

Enjoy!

Bauman (2005) appeared to be on to something, then, when he wrote that there has been a shift from a work ethic to a consumer ethic. A work ethic connected people in their place of employment, where links of common identity could forge a sense of solidarity among workers. A consumer ethic is disconnected from place; there is no common identity or prospect for organised resistance unless the meaning is stretched to include tokenistic consumer boycotts. Marcuse had earlier said that consumerism is the promise of an object that can instantly gratify desire. The immediate 'desublimated' satisfaction of desire had to be paid for in the workplace. The more dependent we were on products for satisfaction, the greater the dependency on employers to provide a wage so that we could afford our piece of satisfaction. The consumer ethic is, in this respect, entirely correlative to the work ethic defined in Chapter 2 as a decentred synthetic ethic of employability. There it was claimed that, by identifying with the 'life outside of work', we satisfy a demand of employers for an independent flourishing spirit who, in its service to society, develops the characteristics employers want.

With the rise of consumer markets, especially after 1945, we see then a shift from a repressive superego that says you cannot enjoy, to the one of Marcuse that says you can enjoy, to the one of Lacan that says you must enjoy. The more that capital depends for its circulation on our consumerist enjoyments, the more important it is for advertisers to channel that desire into the product. The untrammelled desires of consumers show, according to Bauman, that:

> Marcuse's quandary is outdated since 'the individual' has already been granted all the freedom he might have dreamed of and the freedom he might have reasonably hoped for; social institutions are only too willing to cede the worries of definitions and identities to the individual initiative while universal principles to rebel against are hard to find. (2006:22)

But Marcuse, as we noted, insisted that for pleasures to be realised the structures of the reality principle had to be dismantled first. With production under the control of workers, automated technologies could be put to the service of pleasure by allowing for the expansion of free time. In fact, what Bauman describes is simply what Deleuze and Guattari already said about the capitalist axiomatic, that business feeds on decoded flows of desire by recoding it for production and consumption.

Capitalism, according to Deleuze and Guattari, is a unique historical form that relies for its existence on desires that are potentially destructive to it. Capitalism, they say, is the, 'Only social machine that is constructed on the basis of decoded flows. It liberates the flows of desire but under social conditions that define and limit it' (2003:139). In contrast to Freud, desire is productive rather than incestuous; through the progressive stages of Oedipalisation we learn by the phallic stage – related to fears of (symbolic) castration or disempowerment – to feel guilty about our desires and repress them into capitalism's own libidinal economy. As with 1968, the combinatory power of uninhibited desire – a desiring machine – can be potentially revolutionary, but also vulnerable to capture into the capitalist machine with the guilt-inducing feedback loops that turn desire against itself. Desire is something we learn to repress.

Lacan made a similar point to Frankfurt School theorists when claiming that enjoyment is now an obligation, we must enjoy because we can enjoy.[1] In other words, *enjoy!* Lacan is describing a strange kind of enjoyment, though – the pleasure derived from thwarted attempts to possess an object of desire. We can think of this with Todd McGowan's (2004) example of the pleasure children get when opening Christmas presents. Parents often complain that children lose interest once the presents are opened. As a Lacanian would recognise, it is the wrapping not the gift itself that provides the ritualised form of pleasure. Christmas Day would be like any other if the gifts had already been opened. As soon as we get what we want, another object is put in its place, another wrapped present, with only the fantasy of the object of desire contained inside. It is when the objective limit of the wrapping itself is the source of satisfaction that desire turns to drive, hitting against the limit again and again and wanting nothing more. So, in a certain sense, there is nothing beneath the wrapping; a present is simply a present. The product inside cannot satisfy; they at best provide a temporary fix on our desires. McGowan says today we live in a 'society of enjoyment' in which the pursuit of pleasure without inhibition becomes a universal injunction. The superego demands that we sacrifice ourselves to the society of enjoyment. We become indebted consumers trying to satisfy this never satiated demand to enjoy.

Lacan describes three modes of enjoyment. In imaginary enjoyment, the subject visualises a pleasure that the symbolic order prohibits. She falsely recognises in those objects of desire the subversion of prohibitions: the exuberant party of revellers running around town in fancy dress, the worker cocking a snook at his boss while dutifully carrying out the task, the puritan who quaffs a whisky double when no one is looking and the deviant who enjoys multiple sex partners as a mark of her identity and freedom from monogamous constraints. The real transgression, the forbidden object, is always beyond reach. In a Lacanian sense, *Real* enjoyment is the non-symbolic orgasmic disturbance that exhausts itself as soon as it is realised. In its symbolic form, enjoyment is something that occurs elsewhere; it is the other who enjoys. We can think of this by returning to Žižek's description of 'interpassive' enjoyment; a pleasure derived from witnessing someone else's pleasure, such as in television comedies where the canned laughter does the job of laughing on our behalf.[2]

There appear, then, to be no rules in a society based on enjoyment – we simply do as we please, except that every avenue for enjoyment has already been enclosed in that clamshell product, in that open planned office and those phoney subversions. In other words, enjoyment is always conditioned by the practical and symbolic limits of a society governed today in the interests of capital. This freedom in servitude is how we should read Baudrillard when he says in *Impossible Exchange* that,

> Since no one fights over our souls any longer, it is up to us to fight over ourselves, to put our own existences on the line, to be endlessly trying things out and competing in a perpetual, infernal contesting of ourselves – though there is no Last Judgement any more, and there are no longer any real rules. (2001:47)

But is it the case anymore that the superego commands us to enjoy now that the financial crisis has precipitated calls for consumerist restraint?

Enjoy?!

In the previous chapter, I argued that material symptoms of capitalism serve a hegemonic function by their framing as indeterminate problems that we all, in some loosely defined way, are held to be responsible for. Examples were given of the way a culture of crisis industry evokes and manipulates desire to create markets for products with ethical and ecological signifiers. One such example was the Amnesty International campaign to party for human rights. Let us take a closer look at this with another sample from their campaign website (2010):

> Join thousands of others around the country to protect human rights by throwing a party and taking action.

> Parties are the perfect excuse to get friends, neighbours, colleagues – or
> even complete strangers – together in the name of human rights. From
> club nights to clothes swaps, pyjama parties to picnics ... the possibilities
> are endless!

In the Lacanian reading, the injunction to enjoy our freedom presupposes a submission to the symbolic order through our socialisation; it is just that we often do not recognise how our own enjoyments are already coordinated within a socio-economic frame. In this case, however, a more explicit barrier is introduced, that of guilt for enjoying rather than for *not* enjoying. We are only free to enjoy so long as we have served penance. There is a two-fold demand: atone for guilt and enjoy, go forth and gift your guilt, then you are free to multiply your desires. We dispense with guilt by consuming the Amnesty 'product' which permits us to enjoy only when we have confessed to and atoned for our crimes. An ethical alibi is required before uninhibited pleasure can occur. Fundraising is the 'perfect excuse' for a party.

On a recent visit to China, I picked up a magazine that included a column on workplace diplomacy. It advised the Western visitor when speaking with Chinese people to 'beat around the bush', to speak indirectly when disapproving of or rejecting an argument or request. The Westerner should use implied speech instead of more direct forms of communication. Instead of saying, 'No, I can't do this', Chinese people, we learn, would say something like, 'I'll give it my best shot' or, 'Maybe I have time'. The Westerner should read the rejection into the statement. When being critical, instead of saying, 'This is awful, redo it', one should say, 'Not bad, think about it some more'. Failing this, 'Being exaggeratedly indirect, as a joke, can be a great way to show your sensitivity to their culture, and your eagerness to be one with the team' (The World of Chinese 2010). Enjoyment operates according to this principle, except the implied speech is in the question itself: always, 'Would you like to buy chocolate that helps (starving) people in Africa?' and never, 'You must buy Fairtrade chocolate.' Here, however, you are permitted to enjoy upon answering to an offer to gift your guilt and give up a piece of your *jouissance* first.

Consider Disney's Orlando theme park 'Give a Day. Get a Disney Day' programme (Ford 2010). We always have to 'give a day' in order to enjoy a theme park, whether earning the wage that pays for our entry or by labouring in the inevitable queues for rides. Our submission to the order of work and leisure is made complete when 'giving a day' also means atoning for our guilt for being a wage earner and a consumer. As with Product (RED), the superego does not force us to make this choice. Still, we should do as we please and only gift our guilt if we really want to. This qualifies what Lacan says about enjoyment being an injunction to do as we please and guilt being something we feel for not enjoying. In the form of the social logic with its ethical injunctions, we feel guilty for enjoying if we have not earned the privilege to enjoy beforehand.

We pay for our enjoyments with wages of guilt and when penance has been served only then can we really enjoy guilt free. We can have as much dessert as we like, on the condition that we have eaten our dinner first. Have we given a day? Now, enjoy(!). The form of superego injunction changes in place and time. On 15 September 2008, *enjoy!*, as a dominant ideological injunction in Western consumerist societies, became *enjoy?!*

At the time of writing, there are major protests and strikes happening in Greece over the attempt of the government to impose an austerity package that, in the words of Joseph Stiglitz (2010), would force the country into a social and economic death spiral like Argentina a decade before. The argument that most of the media carried was that the Greek people had brought the crisis upon themselves by binging on cheap credit. The consumer had desired too much and read the superego injunction to enjoy too literally. As a commentator for the *Guardian* put it, 'it's time to take the pain as the Irish have, that we did this to ourselves and there's no choice but to put on a brave face and forge a "New Greece".' (Christofer 2010).

So what is a 'New Greece' or, for that matter, a 'new' crisis Europe? With governments across Europe planning/initiating massive cuts in public spending, what is happening in Greece extends across the continent and beyond. The superego returns to put a stop on subjective enjoyment and also on the possibility for countries in Europe, under the rules of monetary policy, to spend their way out of recession.[3] The policy disturbs the affinity between surplus-value and surplus-enjoyment. With the latter denied its consumerist moorings, desire has nowhere left to go. Such a situation cannot endure, either for capital or the subject.

The point of psychoanalysis, writes Žižek (2006:304), is to allow the person *not* to enjoy, to be relieved of the burden of the Other's desire. In the context of spiralling national debt, the other now demands repression of enjoyment; but the other, in the form of capital, cannot survive if desire is crushed. A superego is required that neither prohibits nor commands enjoyment, the kind described here that puts '?' before '!' in the imperative form of the verb to 'enjoy'. There are those who are not permitted to enjoy until they meet certain demands. The immigrant has to earn the right to remain and the unemployed have to provide proof that they are 'actively seeking work' before being permitted welfare payments. Like a beggar on the streets who spends the money given to her on alcohol, in the eyes of society the unemployed should not enjoy until getting out of their predicament. We have been schooled to *enjoy?!* in our quests for employability. Prospects Directory tells us to ask ourselves the following questions:

- What exactly have you done?
- What were you responsible for?
- What were the outcomes?
- How did you achieve success?
- Is there evidence of 'how' you have demonstrated relevant skills?

In the ethical injunction, enjoyment is good for the people and planet. In the enterprise injunction, enjoyment enhances the CV. Enjoy(!) if it looks good on the CV(?). The question posed by the gatekeeper authority, the employer for example, is direct: Have you?/Did you? The ethical injunction, you must give because you can give, is indirect: Would you like? Could you? *People enjoy themselves, but should they?* These are the qualifications for enjoyment, in the one case material and in the other symbolic. In the symbolic form we can refuse to give and in doing so imagine, perhaps, that our refusal is subversive. When ethics is knotted into the code of a gatekeeping authority, refusal to give a little to get a little is not an option.

The form of enjoyment that in different ways Marcuse and Lacan describe is still prevalent; there is, nonetheless, a growing tendency towards a more repressive superego and this has political implications. A superego that demands enjoyment feeds on excess. If that excess can no longer go to the shops, it has to find another outlet. There is a greater potential for desire to find its object in opposition to a system in crisis when it is that system that appears to foreclose the means to enjoy. By learning, once again, to repress our desires, which the ideology on government debt encourages, we are in effect submitting to the performance principle of capitalism in its crisis phase by accepting the need for restraint. It is precisely now that excess has the potential of becoming political, but it can be a politics of the left or the right that captures that excess. In this 'war on excess', an enemy every bit as abstract and absurd as 'terror', the victim is the much maligned working class consumer.

With the economy now in crisis, those who read the superego injunction to enjoy too literally are forced to make the 'hard choices' by doing more to improve employability, and to act in ethically responsible ways to reverse a moral decline precipitated by untrammeled desire. The job is to regulate our desire by servicing our 'debt' to society, a society that for so long has permitted enjoyment because it served the consumerist model of accumulation. We service our debt to ensure the survival of the banking-corporate-liberal parliamentary apparatuses. The carrot on the stick is the prospect that one day we can *enjoy(!)* again. We would have earned it.

Enterprise

Factory of enjoyment

It is not enough simply to have a good time, observed Adorno (2001:191) we need the trophy to prove it. 'If employees return from their holidays without having acquired the mandatory skin tone, they can be quite sure their colleagues will ask them the pointed question, "Haven't you been on holiday then?"'. According to Maurizio Lazzarato (2008:27), the 'dialectics of work and play' have entered into a continuum. It is now possible, he writes, 'to arrange in a thousand different ways the coefficients of work and play, autonomy and subordination, activity and passivity, intellectual and manual labour, which nourish capitalist valorisation.' Rather than link play with societies of control, implied in Lazzarato's point, here I want to focus mainly on the enclosure of play in the workplace factory of enjoyment.

Lasch wrote that,

> Men seek in play the difficulties and demands – both intellectual and physical – they no longer find in work... Work now retains so few traces of play, and the daily routine affords so few opportunities to escape from the ironic self-consciousness that has assumed the quality of a routine, that people seek abandon in play with more than the usual intensity. (1991:101–2)

Far from being devoid of play, the workplace embraces and absorbs it more than ever. Workers demand enjoyment; the firm, in turn, insists on it. Fun, play, pleasure and enjoyment are re-imagined for enterprise.

The character of David Brent in the BBC satire and US spin-off *The Office* (BBC) embodies the fun aesthetic that firms have deployed in recent decades to improve relations between staff and management to create conducive environments for team-based enterprise. While Brent's antics often seem ridiculous, they are not so far-fetched that they undermine the satirical intent. Enterprise creates the playground within the organisation. Fun, says Peter Fleming (2005), has become serious business. Weber's 'rules of separation' between administration and private life is blurred, with employees being encouraged to bring to the workplace practices normally associated with private life. Fleming found in his study of an American-owned UK call centre that its japes and high jinks had, according to some workers, created an environment reminiscent of kindergarten. For others, a fun workplace was a sure sign that management cared about its employees.

Certificates, references, contacts, anecdotes, a personality of a kind, enterprise, ethics and fun all add up to a winning CV. Fun is for the weekend. Fun is what employers demand. As the UK company Softcat (2010) put it: 'Life outside of work is important, our philosophy of work hard and have fun is the life blood of the business'. 'Woe betide you if you have no hobby, no pastime' wrote Adorno (2001:190), or, we can add, woe betide you if you do not share the employer's humour and take part in the fun activities of the firm. Business encloses spaces outside of the time and place of work by already signalling what constitutes purposeful free time, and adapts this injunction into its own practice.

So, in regard to the first point, that leisure is something that takes on the appearance of work, Adorno and Horkheimer claimed that,

> Amusement under late capitalism is the prolongation of work… What happens at work, in the factory, or in the office can only be escaped from by approximation to it in one's leisure time… Pleasure hardens into boredom because, if it is to remain pleasure, it must not demand any effort and therefore moves rigorously in the worn grooves of association. (1997:137)

However, this relationship is today more explicitly related to employment. Promotional literature for gap years illustrates the point that employers demand enjoyment outside of the workplace.[4] A gap year is a period when the more affluent classes choose to take 'time out' from paid labour and formal education to do something seen as productive. The not-for-profit YearOutGroup.org (2010) explains that a gap year,

> can make a big statement about you as a person, both to academics and employers and you know how important that CV is going to be! If properly planned, a year out can say as much, if not more, about you as an individual, as any set of exam results ever can!
> So WHAT you do in YOUR YEAR OUT is VITAL! (original emphasis)

Catherine Casey, writing on a qualitative study she conducted in the firm Hephaestus, claims that the processes of pseudo-individualisation, described by Frankfurt School theorists, are today more sophisticated and less discernible within a new managerial corporate culture. Employees, she says, paradoxically 'derive satisfaction, a sense of relatedness, relative meaningfulness and higher productivity' by participating in the firm's more personalised environment (1995:149). Costea, et al. (2005:150) talk about the 'new alignments between play and self' in the managerial firm. Ideas of 'play-as-work', of 'consumption-as-fun', and so on, redraw the lines of engagement between persons and institutions. Environments are created that 'allow a certain move beyond a sense of organisational domination' to one in which the worker has a sense of 'self-affirmation', 'non-exploitation', 'psychological continuity, and an almost endless pleasure in "being there"'.

An article in the *Sunday Times* reported on the importance of fun in the workplace. 'Fun-sultants' are employed to help company executives make the workplace more attractive to their employees, particularly the younger ones. As one consultant, Laura Ricci (cited in Rushe 2007), interviewed for the piece, explains: 'Management is facing a dilemma with the youth coming out of college. The younger generation have seen the high divorce rates and the stress of their parents' generation. They say that, if you're going to make us spend so much time at work, then you'd better make it fun.' The playground is absorbed into the workplace to make up for the playtime lost to longer working hours. The factory of enjoyment is where the 'factory-less workforce' also enjoys leisure. The *Sunday Times* piece ends with a tip from Gail Hahn's *52 ways to have fun at work* (cited in Rushe 2007):

> Create a surprise celebration. Celebrate the uncelebrated – Mondays. What better day than Monday to start things off right. Have a bit of fun at the beginning of the day, at the beginning of the week. After meeting a sales goal, landing a big account or exceeding production expectations the previous week, let all the employees know that on Monday you will be bringing a special treat. Start the week off with some fun to pump up morale and boost productivity.

On condition that productivity goals are met, the employer permits the worker their piece of *jouissance*. The superego injunction to enjoy takes on a more direct form when demanded by the actual employer. Those who do enjoy, or feign enjoyment, answer in the affirmative when asked the question 'are you a team player?' The presupposition of management that company pranks are universally welcome is entirely understandable if McGowan is right that indeed we do live in a culture of enjoyment, at least within more affluent societies.

Fun militates against the mundane, exhausting, alienating, dispiriting and disempowering nature of employment. The Fun at Work Company caters for our needs by providing business with a few good ideas on how to drain from us the residue of pleasure reserved for outside the workplace. The Fun at Work Café (2010) has a list of 'wow' ideas, 'physical fun', 'cerebral stuff', 'jokes and japes', 'wellbeing' and 'themed events' for the corporate executive to choose from. Why not 'Surprise and amuse your staff, charm your visitors with your new "trainee" receptionist', dolled up to look like a third-rate impersonator of a celebrity. 'Prices start from just £500'. How about 'Gorilla Hunt', one of the 'more bizarre and wacky in house jokes [sic].' This one involves 'realistic' looking gorillas moving into the workplace; presumably not too realistic, though. For a 'WOW!' activity 'guaranteed to raise a smile as well as some oohs and ahhs' cover the exterior of the workplace in false snow and pump snowflakes past the windows. 'Book early just to be sure!' And if all this fails try out the 'laughter clinic':

> You've seen the mickey taking on the TV ... but we all agree that laughter is the best cure for just about every problem... We just need some help to let go. These classes are just so fun, invigorating and energising. Why let happiness be hostage to occasional happenstance . Organised at your convenience ... go for it and have a real laugh. (Fun at Work Company, 2010)

Note the attempt to defuse the obvious association with *The Office*. Still not smiling? How about a 'smile workshop' to help you lighten up?

A smile costs nothing and makes everybodys [sic] day ... but have some of us forgotten how? Our theatre director will teach your staff that 'natural' smile without the cheesy grin. These are fun workshops that everyone can enjoy. (Fun at Work Company, 2010)

With branches around the world, The Team Building Directory (2010) provides sober advice on how to create a fun working environment. 'Thinking of taking a day off?', they ask, 'Forget it! If you want more hilarity than you can handle, then work is the place to be!' Their ideas of fun are similar to the Fun at Work Company. In 'Boss Tennis' the 'boss is the "ball"... once he's finished with you, you must send (volley) him to someone on the other side of the room.' Boss football would be more fun. Then there is 'Engaged' which, hilariously, involves getting 'hold of as many pairs of boots or shoes and trousers as you can' and arranging them in toilet cubicles to 'watch the queue grow' outside them, a certifiable offence in any other situation. With more fun than one can handle, the emotional reserves of pleasure are exhausted and a holiday from fun would be called for, if holidays were not already boot camps of enjoyment.

Did Adorno really anticipate this configuration of enterprise and enjoyment? Had Marcuse this in mind when describing the happy consciousness? Is this what Christopher Lasch was hoping for when complaining that work had become divorced from play? Will psychoanalysis help to relieve us of the burden to enjoy? It seems unlikely.

So what about the cynic? As Todd McGowan reminds us, the person not taken in by the bluff does not see reality but instead mistakes what they take for reality as reality itself. We cannot escape the symbolic order in which consciousness is trapped. We are duped and sometimes we do not know it. The same holds for strategies to resist workplace fun. Wearing an excessive smile might make the job more tolerable, but it does not change the fact that we nonetheless smile. In the factory of enjoyment there is no alternative to smiling.

This is why the advice of sites such as The Fun at Work Café (2010), providing tips on how to make work fun by getting one over on the employer, backfires. The site advertises a number of publications on this theme. The main page opens with the following:

> No matter how intense your boredom, doing one or more of the following top ten fun things to do at work should help kill your boredom at your workplace without you having to resort to a gun.

This includes pretending 'that you are working when you aren't – just like you are doing right now!'; generating 'symptoms of severe psychological abuse which you can then blame on your boss'; or sending 'a memo to everyone in the office stating that you have heard a rumour that someone has a crush on you and you would like to find out who it is'. Such 'tips' are unlikely to be carried through if the person wants to maintain a positive relationship with their colleagues and keep their job, or has any interest in maintaining a service that customers are likely to depend on. The site advertises books 'on how you can leverage your how-to advice on any topic and make a fortune at it so that you can leave your boring job and never have to feel imprisoned again'(The Fun at Work Cafe, 2010). Whereas the Fun at Work Company promises a fun workplace, this site offers the fantasy of fun at work for those in the know, turning imaginary subversion into an enterprise.

Work and leisure are more than ever a false dichotomy. Work expands into the world of leisure, while leisure expands into the world of work. When work is dehumanised, writes István Mészáros, 'self-fulfilment achieved through labour as man's life-activity is unthinkable.' (2005:263) What is left is a 'dehumanised illusion of fulfilment through "withdrawal", through "contemplative" idleness, through the cult of "privacy", "irrationality", and "mysticism"'. Humanised companies are the standard bearer of what it means to be human; they create a 'dehumanised illusion of fulfilment' at the site of exploitation. Huizinga (1992:7) wrote that 'First and foremost... all play is a voluntary activity. Play to order is no longer play: it could at best be but a forcible imitation of it.' Homo ludens has become an abstract quantity of capital, with the culture industry firmly rooted in the factory of enjoyment. Perhaps the new personality of our time is the Homo Vacuus, the blank canvas on to which fun is painted.

Undimensional man

There has been a growth, Sennett wrote, of a common personality that derives its social character from public life. Its actual social connections are weak while its group identity, sustained through acts of fantasy, is strong yet inherently unstable. The fascination with celebrity is an example of this. People do not generally have a connection in their social lives with celebrities. This does not prevent us, though, from harbouring fantasies about our inner connections to them, as was the case with the death of Princess Diana and, as widely reported, people grieving for her more than when close family members died. Sennett (2002) called this connection a phantasmal community or 'destructive Gemeinschaft'. Christopher Lasch had a similar understanding of where society was heading. The narcissistic personality is a character, he said, who constantly seeks confirmation from the mass media and others of their grandiose self-image. The media, '[G]ive substance to and thus intensify narcissistic dreams of fame and glory, encourage the common man to identify himself with the stars and to hate the "herd," and to make it more and more difficult for him to accept the banality of everyday existence.' (Lasch 1991:21) What could be called the undimensional wo/man[5] of our time overcomes feelings of insecurity by attaching herself to those who radiate nothing in particular, such as the ordinary celebrity of reality television.

With echoes of Richard Sennett's destructive *Gemeinschaft* thesis, Chris Rojek (2001:187–8) argues that recent media preoccupations with celebrity are in part an attempt to achieve subjective integration, 'not by unifying the alienated parts of personality, but by subsuming alienated personality to the "greater whole" of the public face of celebrity.' In a Durkheimian lexicon, celebrity is the totem providing the form into which an alienated public can insert its fantasies. Those who recognise, worship and, equally, despise celebrities accord them symbolic power. When this relationship comes to an end, the celebrity fades from public view. Celebrities are our ideal-egos, our role models showing us how to consume.

The cynic likes to see the celebrity fall from grace to confirm the emptiness beneath the veneer. But the cynic's work is already done for them. If once celebrities had specific qualities or talents that marked them out from the crowd, today the celebrity is increasingly distinguished by their ordinariness. We are shown that there really is nothing beneath the surface. This is the novelty running counter to the once dominant image of celebrity glamour. Lasch had also anticipated this,

> The urge to understand a magician's tricks, like the recent interest in the special effects behind a movie like *Star Wars*, shares with the study of literature a willingness to learn from the masters of illusion lessons about reality itself. But a complete indifference even to the mechanics of illusion announces the collapse of the very idea of reality, dependent at every point on the distinction between nature and artifice, reality and illusion. This indifference betrays the erosion of the capacity to take any interest in anything outside the self. Thus the worldly child, unmoved, stuffs herself with cotton candy and 'wouldn't care' even if she knew how twenty-four clowns fit into a single car. (1991:89)

What this misses, however, is the point Žižek makes about pseudo-transparency using the same example of the 'paradigmatic case' of 'making of...' films,

> [F]ar from destroying the 'fetishist' illusion, the insight into the production mechanism in fact even strengthens it, in so far as it renders palpable the gap between the bodily causes and the surface-effect... In short, the paradox of 'the making of...' is the same as that of a magician who discloses the trick without dissolving the mystery of the magical effect. (1997:102)

What is not so readily appreciated is that the revelation is in itself the mechanism that binds us to the symbolic order. In 1991, at the height of her career, the pop star Madonna commissioned a fly-on-the-wall documentary, *In Bed with Madonna* (dir. Alex Keshishian, 1991), in which over the course of a year a camera recorded her in her daily life. The message of the documentary was a now familiar one, that beneath all the glamour, the magic, there is a normal vulnerable individual. Television shows such as *Big Brother* (Endemol) and documentaries on the daily lives of ordinary people are an extension of this. The difference being that there is no magic to unmask in the first place. Television is the little boy pointing out that there are no clothes and in doing so creates out of ordinariness a more transparent form of clothing, analogous to the effect of nylon hosiery referred to in the previous chapter. In public displays of ordinary lives, Couldry (2002:288) writes, 'insofar as it was "ordinary," this *was* the reality that would exist without the media being there.' Our TV specs are so saturated with images of celebrities that the plain itself has the capacity to become novel, magical even: taking on a shine. And in this case we also wear the hosiery, becoming the undifferentiated mirror of the naked celebrity. The unremarkable becomes remarkable when it is stitched into a visual spectacle that fetishises nobody in particular. Undimensional man is the subject of end-capitalism who signifies nothing as content. And where nothingness is mediatised the form itself has the appearance of content.

Adorno (2000:100–1) described the celebrity a brand-name commodity, 'alien and incomprehensible to themselves, and, as their own living images, they are as if dead.' The ordinary star of reality television represents a celebration of nothingness or perhaps even a celebration of an uncanny, neither dead nor alive, apparition of the general public. In his well-known essay on the uncanny, Freud (2003) noted how children in early play make no distinction between animate and inanimate objects. The uncanny double is a thing reminiscent of us, but is not quite there, and it is this proximity to the real that lends it a ghoulish quality. We see this uncanny object in representations of humans in videogames. And there is something ghoulish about computer-generated imagery (CGI) rendered children's characters in films such as *Shrek* (dir. Andrew Adamson & Vicky Jenson, 2001) and *Kung Fu Panda* (dir. Mark Osborne & John Stevenson, 2008). Their appeal parallels the popularity of the uncanny represen-tations of undimensionality in television shows. The narcissist, in identifying with the undimensional screen double, sees the reflection of her own neither dead nor alive self. As culture is infantilised, the difference between the animate and inanimate is once again blurred and the subject who withdraws into this primitive form of narcissism sees in the reality television star, or the ghoulish anthropomorphic CGI character, a reflection of nothing. The emptiness at the core of celebrity, and by extension our subjectivity, both fascinates and revolts us.

If nothingness is passively consumed when watching television, becoming undimensional is elsewhere an active endeavour. Such is the case with the online social networking site Facebook with its predetermined form into which standardised portraits and profiles are inserted. Here nothingness is the positive substance designed to appeal to casual and intimate friends alike, including those once forgotten now forever renewed with each refreshing of the page. On Facebook the user feels obliged to respond to the endless requests to join groups where commonality is established at the most generic of levels; here also is a live feed of information on what friends are about to have for dinner – *roasties, perhaps?* – or the historical figure friends most resemble – *Joan of Arc?* The banality is intoxicating, if only to marvel at how far the culture industry has evolved. We see a similar phenomenon on dating sites where profiles are emptied of any substance that might create the 'wrong impression'. In the quest for undimensional love, nothing should reflect nothing where the generic bait or tagline are variations on 'likes to have fun' or 'doesn't take life too seriously'.

Whatever the fantasy of fame, the evanescence marking the slide into undimensionality responds to the same desire to be desired in a world where nothingness is elevated to the level of fetish. We seek to mimic the ghoulish apparitions of normality in order to be likeable to others. The Facebook friend is like Adorno and Horkheimer's (1997:155) 'modern city-dweller who can now only imagine friendship as a "social contact": that is, as being in social contact with others with whom he has no inward contact.' In an inverse relationship, the more Facebook friends we have, the more pressure there is to fit into a generic profile where attitude is signified according to whether or not we tag a 'thumbs up' to a message or video clip a friend has inserted on the site.

There is no 'thumbs down'. The most clichéd of profiles become the most popular, a direct corollary of the homogenisation the culture industry promotes or the big Boss demands and capital, in sum, relies on to smooth out the antagonisms that cut through it.

'Being nothing is intoxicating,' asserts Pessoa quoted in Baudrillard (2001:54), 'and the will is a bucket you knocked over in the yard, with a lazy flick of the foot, as you went by'. This is Nietzsche's will to nothingness:

> this hate of the human, and even more of the animal, and more still of the material, this horror of the senses, of reason itself, this fear of happiness and beauty, this desire to get right away from all illusion, change, growth, death, wishing and even desiring – all this means – let us have the courage to grasp it – a will to Nothingness, a will opposed to life, a repudiation of the most fundamental conditions of life, but it is and remains *a will!* – and to say at the end that which I said at the beginning – man will wish *Nothingness* rather than not wish at all. (2003:118)

The will to nothingness is therefore an active endeavour; we become undimensional not by depriving the senses, but rather by marshalling them in the service of the established gatekeepers of what it means to be human today. Whether it is the cynic who self-consciously wills nothing or those who simply try to fit in, the outcome is the same, the death of the personality in the eviscerated zones of work and play superadded with enterprise, ethics and enjoyment.

Becoming an undimensional or generic personality is an enterprise in itself. Substance has to be removed or hidden from view and replaced by a different kind of character whose show of personality reproduces subjectivity at the level of cliché. The nakedness is the canvas on to which the other can apply its brush strokes, such as on Facebook where the user inserts content into the empty frames of the site in anticipation of what the other wants. Blanks are filled in with blanks.

The advice given on house makeover programmes is illustrative here. In the *House Doctor* (Talkback Productions) format, the hapless seller is shown videos of prospective buyers looking around and commenting negatively on their property. The programme's presenter then advises on how to make the house more sellable. This involves 'keeping it neutral' by removing any traces of personality and turning the home, in their words, into a 'blank canvas'. The same also goes for the much sought after 'character property' removed of any clutter that might cause offence.[6] The blank canvas is the frame into which the content of enterprise, ethics and enjoyment entwine. Dynamism, conscientiousness and joy imbricate at the points of nothingness in the un/conscious will to become undimensional.

Ethics

Carnivalesque in absentia

If in the past it was possible to avoid having fun simply by not entering the social club, disco or bar where fun was expected of you, now fun is omnipresent and inescapable. Fun intrudes upon 'free time', workplace and life generally. For every situation there is the bore making light of, and in subtle ways policing, conversation in case it gets too serious. A feigned smile or forced chuckle is often necessary to satisfy the group, the staged responses in every day life that Erving Goffman described. When fun is too much bother we can enjoy it vicariously by watching repeats of television comedy. And in an age when the inelegant and inarticulate garble found on text messages, blogs, internet forums and live streams is so easy to misinterpret, the smiley is at hand to serve as the instant multipurpose fix to assure its reader of the harmless intention. Even the most joyless of organisations – the British Conservative Party – are in on the act. In the lead-up to the 2010 general election, members of the Conservative Party were encouraged to run 'watch parties' during the live television debates of the leading contenders. A website was set up to guide people on how to run them. 'It's completely up to you how you do it', it advises (Conservatives 2010). 'You could just invite some friends to gather around your TV over pizza, or you could arrange an organised evening that is open to a large number of people.' But '[F]irst and foremost, your Watch Party should be fun.'

There are sound strategic reasons for introducing a fun dimension to ethical campaigns. Oxfam (2010), for example, encouraged children in Darfur's refugee camps to maintain basic hygiene by making cleansing 'serious fun'. For all its cynicism, Amnesty's 'Party For Human Rights' campaign recognises that fun is likely to attract new sponsors. It is a realistic expectation. In a non-ironic but self-conscious way, fun can be introduced into political protest to humanise resistance, to create a disjunction between an image – say of a clown – and ugly violence of police oppression.[7] Such protests are sometimes described as 'carnivalesque'. This term comes from the Russian literary critic Mikhail Bakhtin. But his definition was rather precise. In carnival, he said,

> everyone is an active participant, everyone communes in the carnival act. Carnival is not contemplated and, strictly speaking, not even performed; its participants *live* in it, they live by its laws as long as those laws are in effect; that is, they live a *carnivalistic life*. Because carnivalistic life is life drawn out of its *usual* rut, it is to some extent 'life turned inside out,' 'the reverse side of the world.' (1984:122)

The carnivalesque is a momentary pause in the law, closer to real non-symbolic enjoyment than the ethical act which attempts to break with law altogether. In the preferred interpretation of postmodernists, the carnivalesque is a colourful display of an exuberant, often affluent, youth, motivated by slogans such as, 'Not in My Name'. In the left-liberal version of the carnivalesque, protest is undimensional: humour and fun defuse politics through alternations of enjoyment and ethics: party for human rights, human rights for party. Citing Berman's *Dark Ages of America,* Langman and Ryan (2009:479) claim that today we are witness to the rebirth of the carnival in a mass mediated form that engenders a common 'carnival character' social type. As Bakhtin had observed, modern forms of comedy and satire allow for no prospect of change. This form of the carnivalesque is a staged excess of law announcing, like a pupil whose absence is noted by the teacher on a class register, the carnivalesque in absentia.

According to Robert Westwood, humour serves a range of objectives, 'stimulating creativity, improving decision-making, enhancing morale, improving group functioning, or cementing cultural values' (2004:776). Comedy, he says, 'is primarily a subversive reminder, an echo of subversive possibilities, rather than something that ultimately can *perform* subversively'. (Westwood 2004: 785) The BBC's bi-annual television charity-athon *Comic Relief*, with smaller versions in the United States, Australia and elsewhere, is probably the most inclusive and extensive festival of fun in the UK.[8] It brings politicians, business leaders, celebrities and the general public together in support of a cause; whether the cause in question is ethics or enjoyment is uncertain. The idea is for members of the public to raise money leading up to 'Red Nose Day' when the show is broadcast on television. Filled with comic sketches and appeals for money from celebrities, the show lasts the entire evening. Other broadcasters acknowledge the importance of the event by removing from their schedules shows that might draw audiences away. The studio serves as the 'nerve centre' of comedy/ethics, with telephone operators seen at the back of the studio to remind us that others are donating while the show is being aired. Like a ticker tape at the bottom of the screen, messages of support and examples of public and celebrity generosity also encourage the viewer to donate. The website provides us with the best summary of what *Comic Relief* is about:

> Red Nose Day culminates in a night of hilarious comedy and moving documentary films on BBC One – it's a night when the only place to be is right in front of the TV screen. Tune in on Friday, from 7pm, BBC One to Comic Relief. All this funny business unites the whole nation in trying to make a difference to the lives of thousands of people living in abject poverty, or facing terrible injustice, both across Africa and in the UK.

Humour becomes a conservative reaction formation that takes the edge out of images of inequality and injustice. At the same time that it responds to a need to do away with the unpleasant images of another's suffering, it allows for opportunities, in this case, to dress up, conduct pranks, party and transform schools, hospitals, workplaces and city streets into fundraising playpens:

> In schools, offices and homes across the land, everyone wears – you've guessed it – the latest Red Nose… and does whatever tickles their fancy to raise cash. You name it, they do it! From sponsored kissathons and flamboyant fancy dress to gungetastic [sic.] trials and naked pole vaulting. Ok, we made the last one up. (BBC 2009a)

And here we find the most unlikely of bedfellows, an enterprising interpassive:

> If you'd rather raise some money from the comfort of your own armchair, try one of these relaxing ideas: (i) 'Watch something funny' – invite your mates round and watch some classic comedy films. Charge for the comfiest seats and sell refreshments; and (ii) 'Play something funny' – invite your friends round and get out all your old board games, or how about a few hands of your favourite card games. (BBC 2009a)

It is an entire nation of the carnivalesque in absentia, the idiot court jester forced to be king for a day, forced to demonstrate a conscience, a fun loving personality and commitment to the team. It is the perfect excuse for the factory of enjoyment to promote an ethical image of itself. Politicians can also use the event to improve their public profile. For example, Tony Blair, when Prime Minister at the height of the Iraq conflict in 2005, appeared in a sketch with the then popular comedienne Catherine Tate as part of the fundraising exercise.[9] It is a nation that gifts its guilt. 'Thank you for helping us to change lives', the site said (BBC 2009b) after the 2009 event. 'You have helped us to raise an incredible… £82.3 million.'

Comic Relief embodies and universalises the three injunctions of enterprise, ethics and enjoyment:

> If you love to party then there's loads of ways you can raise some cash whilst having a ball. Ask your friends to pay to party and sell refreshments too… Your cash will give thousands of people who face discrimination, injustice or grinding poverty the chance to transform their lives. (BBC 2009a)

The official partners include the supermarket chain Sainsbury's, Subway and Mini Babybel; supporting partners include Oxfam, Jammie Dodgers (biscuits), Foxy Bingo and the Department for

International Development; the Fairtrade partners are Dubble Chocolate, Liberation and Union Coffee (Red Nose Day 2010). The event circulates images of poverty for the culture of crisis industry to manipulate. It fills in for any lean period when there are no earthquakes, hurricanes or famines to affect sympathy towards. Fun in this respect is totally administered. Enjoyment is the economy of pleasure, a capitalist performance principle, an instrumental-rational-activity and a celebration of the undimensional man who wills a generic space for the carnivalesque in absentia.

iCommunism

When consumption becomes the principal expression of desire, an Apple product becomes an expression of human enjoyment. The problem is not with the product itself, but, as Marx put it, 'a definite production' that 'determines a definite consumption, distribution and exchange as well as *definite relations between these different moments.*' (1973:99) Human desire does not in itself destroy the planet or condemn entire nations to poverty.

Jim McGuigan (2009) writes that for capitalism 'to command hearts and minds, it is necessary to mask out its much less appealing back region', which it does through the marketing of cool. From images of Che Guevara on billboards advertising cars (Ads of the World 2010) to bar chains using symbols of the Russian Revolution (Pravda Vodka Bar 2010), capitalism has long been adept in appropriating forms of counter-cultural politics, art and so forth into signs, symbols and words that sell product. Pierre Bourdieu (2003) noted how the different symbolic values of cultural goods are reflected in the power imbalances in society. Those with access to 'cultural capital' are able to command status and gain entry into privileged social circles. Sarah Thornton (1995) extended this thesis to groups on the margins of society in possession of their own symbolic capital or 'subcultural capital' as she puts it. For Marcuse this would all be part of the one-dimensional brew:

The reign of such a one-dimensional reality does not mean that materialism rules, and that the spiritual, metaphysical, and bohemian occupations are petering out. On the contrary, there is a great deal of "Worship together this week," "Why not try God," Zen, existentialism, and beat ways of life, etc. But such modes of protest and transcendence are no longer contradictory to the status quo and no longer negative. They are rather the ceremonial part of practical behaviourism, its harmless negation, and are quickly digested by the status quo as part of its healthy diet. (2002:16)

To McGuigan (2009:47), Marcuse's view that the incorporation of contradictory symbols into everyday commercial life helped create the dull happy consciousness is 'far too totalising'. Art, after all, is sometimes incompatible in its content to bourgeois appropriation, thus retaining its subversive value (McGuigan 2009:47). So there is always the excess that 'sticks out' and upsets the smooth surface of the all-inclusive culture, and as Deleuze and Guattari emphasised, the very excess is what the axiom of capitalism thrives on. What gets mass produced, though, is not the excess itself, but what has already been captured and turned into a commodity, the thing that was once excessive or non-commodified. What distinguishes cool products is that they have already captured the excess at the moment it reveals itself as such. Cool is the fresh vegetable at the farmer's market. This is what the i of Apple stands for. Unlike the Nike 'swoosh' which, as Naomi Klein (2007) pointed out, is worth more than the company's limited material holdings, the i itself cannot be copyrighted. It is only when the non-commodified excessive i attaches itself limpet-style to another, the Pod or perhaps even Communism, that the thing becomes a sellable brand. We need to split the i from the Pod, to rescue the tunes from their container.

The monetary sign of enjoyment attached to every product is that magical thing or X that promises fulfilment, the brand, the cool, the 'i' that sells the iPhone. This sign, the i of excess, the i of ego, the i for the good times, is transferrable to the workplace where fun becomes a moral issue, the sign of a socially developed and conscientious worker, the iWorker, the iFactory, iGoogle. But excess, as Deleuze and Guattari recognised, is also vital to human life, whether we are talking about the revolutionary act, individual creation, play or pleasure. The i of iPod, the i with exchange-value formerly excess, needs to be returned to its sender and valued on its own terms. The excess currently persists and is re-presented only as a promise of a freedom from the iron cage.

The image of communism is pregnant with random brutality, repression, austerity and cultural asceticism. The idea of communism, as Alain Badiou argues, needs reimagining for the twenty-first century. For a society hung over on enjoyment, communism should also signify pleasure, uninhibited by work or monetary constraint. Perhaps there is a dialectical aspect to the kind of consumerist individualism that many social commentators have despaired of. There is hope in the excess of consumerism if it is split from its commodified moorings, the i without the Pod, the cool without the capitalism, the iCommunism.

Returning to an earlier point, what if capitalism has gone too far in liberating desire? Where material realities today inhibit access to the very products that enjoyment hinges on, desire has neither work nor consumption to exhaust itself in. The use-values of commodities, including their aesthetic/fetishistic qualities, is what communism realises, an idea of society that does not inhibit enjoyment, nor punish the individual for the pleasures derived from a non-commodified consumption, nor enclose and block pleasure except to those who can afford it. The ascetic dreams of the future, tacitly endorsed in moralising forms of socialism and in certain strands of the environmental movement, are as dystopian as anything science fiction has come up with. A non-commodified pleasure, the excess of human existence, as Marcuse recognised, is an ideal worth fighting for. Goran Therborn (2008:64) makes this call:

> The meaning of Marxian Communism was human enjoyment, phrased in terms of a nineteenth-century bucolic ideal. The austerity of the revolutionary struggle substituted a revolutionary heroism for Marxian hedonism, and the latter did not appeal to the 'respectable workers' of social democracy. But after May 1968, the hedonistic, the *ludic*, the playful orientation of the Marxian original must reaffirm its importance.

Within the current constraints of capitalism, the kind of 'society of enjoyment' that Therborn advocates is already rationalised. For a society of 'sustainable' excess, an excessive political act is first required, an excess that cannot be captured. iCommunism is the sign for productive, revolutionary excess: a free activity, pleasure as a guiding principle for the fulfilment of universal justice and equality. iCommunism stands against the politics of austerity, but it is a modus operandi that ultimately requires a different mode of production to universalise it.

Conclusion

This chapter has brought together the final pieces of the enterprise, ethics and enjoyment jigsaw. The chapter imbricates and reinforces arguments of previous chapters on enterprise and ethics. It has elaborated on the play motif in consumption, work and politics. Examples were given of the factory of enjoyment, where exploitation and comedy come together in a nightmarish world with all the appearance of the ludic and the iron fist of enterprise that capitalism demands. Work and leisure extend into one another's spheres rendering the idea of a duality between the two more redundant than ever. The cult of the ordinary, mediated on television and social networking sites, operates like a mirror to reflect a new ideal-type, the undimensional wo/man to whom everyone gives the thumbs up. The image reproduces the vapid trinkets of personality the culture industry thrusts into the limelight. The blank canvas is open to inscription, and re-inscription, into the factory of enjoyment reproduced as carnivalesque in absentia.

Desire has to go somewhere and if it cannot go to the shops or the workplace, whether because of monetary debts or unemployment, the machine of surplus-value risks dissolving its connection to the surplus-enjoyment of consuming subjects. The superego reasserts itself by admonishing us all for enjoying too much, raising a question that qualifies enjoyment without altogether inhibiting it. Now is not the time to tighten our belts. It is the time to punish capitalism's excess.

So where now for enjoyment? As with the chapters on enterprise and ethics, the issue centres on the symbolic composition of the thing we strive to possess – what stands in as the object of desire – and how that thing relates to surplus-value. Enjoyment is not in itself the problem, rather the particular form it takes in latter-day capitalism with regard to the commodified objects we strive to possess. Enjoyment is increasingly a necessity bound to the needs of capital. Fun, pleasure, play and enjoyment are also vital components of human life. They can be tactically subversive when deployed against mechanisms of domination and control. And as Marcuse illustrated, they can be thought as principles underpinning a future liberated society and therein present a vision of communism far removed from the ascetic 'really existing socialism' our imaginations are saturated with. If communism stands for equality, justice and non-alienated labour, it should also stand for pleasure.

6

NAKED ECOLOGY

The science is practically unanimous; the rapid increase in global temperatures, destruction of the ozone layer, quantities of carbon dioxide in the air and in the oceans, and all the charted consequences, from melting ice caps to extreme weather, is in part caused by human intervention. It is rational science that forewarns the apocalypse and simply doing nothing to change the way we live will bring it on. As Anthony Giddens (2009:228) puts it, 'Doomsday is no longer a religious concept, a day of spiritual reckoning, but a possibility imminent in our society and economy.' However, we should be clear from the outset that it is not the individual, as such, that causes climate change but, more specifically, a mode of production that survives by the unrelenting and irrational extraction of vital natural resources used, by necessity, to supply an endless quantity of disposable products for consumers to purchase.

While there was knowledge of the effects of pollution on the ecosystem back in the 1950s, it was not until the 1980s that there was definitive evidence that the burning of fossil fuels was contributing to global warming. The 2007 IPCC report on climate change[1] concluded that human influences had,

- *very likely* contributed to sea level rise during the latter half of the 20th century;
- *likely* contributed to changes in wind patterns, affecting extra-tropical storm tracks and temperature patterns;
- *likely* increased temperatures of extreme hot nights, cold nights and cold days;

- *more likely than not* increased risk of heat waves, area affected by drought since the 1970s and frequency of heavy precipitation events. (IPCC 2007)

Naomi Oreskes (2004) examined the abstracts of 928 peer reviewed scientific papers published between 1993 and 2003, and found unanimity among scientists with regard to the human causes. As the IPCC 2007 report states, 'There is *very high confidence* that the net effect of human activities since 1750 has been one of warming.' [Emphasis added]. The 2006 Stern report commissioned by the British government concluded that an increase of global temperatures of just 2 degrees centigrade could lead to the extinction of between 15% and 40% of all species (Osborne 2006). There is also the widely-mooted danger that the ecosystem is close to a 'tipping point' beyond which the effects would be both unpredictable and likely catastrophic for the entire ecology. Herbert Marcuse (2002:149) wrote of the mathematics of insanity, citing calculations of the number of casualties from a nuclear attack as one example. There is a similar rationalisation of insanity in the calculation of the effects of global warming on the economy, human species and ecosystem. It is the mathematics of insanity when these figures are factored against the preservation of the social relations to calculate how much devastation is tolerable to the economy.

The 1992 Rio Earth Summit, 1997 Kyoto conference, G8 meeting in Rostock in the summer of 2007 and, more recently, the 2009 Copenhagen climate conference attest to the broad consensus on climate change at the governmental level. Public scepticism and apathy remain high though. A potpourri of conspiracy theories, distrust of scientific evidence, the numbing effect of postmodern relativism on political discourse, cynicism and obscurantist dreams of a simpler feudal life feed the scepticism and apathy of a popular backlash (for figures on scepticism, see Goldenberg 2010). There is also a metonymic shift from capitalism to words such as 'industrialisation', 'deforestation' and 'consumer waste' that defuse and depoliticise the cause. In short, there is an ideological vacuum at the heart of the climate change debate for apocalyptic visions of the future to fill. It is good business and, Erik Swyngedouw (2010) claims, a 'decidedly populist' discourse. Populism, writes Slavoj Žižek,

> occurs when a series of particular 'democratic' demands [in this case, a good environment, a retro-fitted climate, a series of socio-environmentally mitigating actions] is enchained in a series of equivalences, and this enchainment produces 'people' as the universal political subject... and all different particular struggles and antagonisms appear as part of a global antagonistic struggle between 'us' (people) and 'them' [in this case 'it' is CO_2]. (cited in Swyngedouw 2010:221)

CO_2, 'it', *objet petit a*, 'thing-like object cause' of climate change, is the reified commodity of carbon trading schemes. The ideology, Swynedouw notes (2010:228–9), presents climate change as a threat to all of humankind without differentiating the more significant consequences for the poor. The threat of nature is externalised as an object that metes its revenge for crimes humanity has committed against it. Criticism is deflected from the internal socio-economic relations at the centre of the problem to the individuals, businesses and nations charged with not doing enough to reduce their carbon footprints. Whereas for socialist movements capitalism is the object cause of inequality, in the climate change discourse there is no other to oppose and so, Swynedow argues, there is no political subject called into being. Carbon neutral is politically neutered.

The only option left is to plead with our leaders to invest in fuel efficient technologies and set limits on the burning of fossil fuels. On 1 January 2009, the *Guardian* newspaper ran an editorial with a letter written by James and Anniek Hansen addressed to Michelle and Barack Obama pleading, in a slightly ironic tone, for help, 'your personal attention to these "details" could make all the difference in what surely will be the most important matter of our times', it read (Hansen & Hansen 2009). The crisis to end all crises is on the horizon and the most we seem willing or able to do is plead to the better conscience of our parliamentary leaders.

Climate change is a hegemonic discourse infused with a left-liberal ideology. This chapter is organised around some of the key concepts developed in previous chapters eschewing the enterprise, ethics and enjoyment structure in favour of a more synthetic approach to this singular issue.

You Can't Stop the Dancing Chicken

What goes for capitalism goes for chickens. Ian Curtis, the lead singer of the cult 1980s band Joy Division, committed suicide after watching Werner Herzog's 1977 *Stroszek*, a film about a German immigrant trying and failing to make ends meet while living in the United States. The film concludes with an iconic sequence of a chicken dancing in a macabre penny amusement. Placing the coin in the machine causes the chicken to peck at a device presumably containing nutrients. The device seems to trigger emissions of electric currents from the floor of the cage causing the chicken to 'dance'. We soon discover that the amusement does not switch off and so the chicken keeps pecking and dancing. This is how Herzog explains his interest in chickens:

> Well they are very frightening for me because their stupidity is so flat. You look into the eyes of a chicken and you lose yourself in a completely flat, frightening stupidity. They are like a great metaphor for me... I kind of love chickens, but they frighten me more than any other animal.
>
> Werner Herzog, commenting on *Stroszek* (1977)

As Chris Harman (2009:310) said of capitalism and climate change, 'Watching such behaviour is a bit like watching a car crash in slow motion, with the driver aware of disaster ahead but ploughing on regardless'. The Marxist solution is to turn the amusement off and free the chicken from the box. The left-liberal solution is to persuade the chicken to peck less frequently; it must dance because it can dance, though not so frantically, it must *enjoy?!*

Ecological Marxists often talk about a nature-society 'metabolism'. The more capitalism develops, the more it 'saps the original source of all wealth: the soil and the labourer' (Becker & Jahn 1998:68). This reaches a point when the natural metabolism between people and nature, organisms and systems collapse (Foster 1999:2000), causing what has been called a 'metabolic rift'. In other words, capitalism with its ever-expanding production violates the social metabolism of reproductive labour creating 'irreparable rifts' in the planetary metabolism of which humans are a part (Clausen & Clark 2005; Foster 1997).

The 'treadmill of production' theory develops from the work of Allan Schnaiberg. This approach stresses the relationship between capital and the state in the tussle to contain the effects of production on the planet. The problem lies in the difficulty of replacing the 'treadmill' of capital-intensive methods of accumulation. Incapable of instituting fundamental change, the most the 'environmental state' appears to do is regulate symptoms of capitalist growth such as pollution and take measures to encourage the use of renewable resources (Mol & Buttel 2002; Schnaiberg, et al. 2002). With an emphasis on profit, sustainability has become the most salient term in mainstream environmental discourse, a discourse on the sustainability of capitalism.

For all the reports on global warming and international conferences setting targets on carbon dioxide emissions, capitalism continues inexorably in its destruction of the global commons. According to international non-profit organisation Global Footprint Network, in 1960 just over half of the planet's resources were needed to supply the 'ecological footprint' of humanity. By 2005, the number was approaching one and half planets (Global Footprint Network 2010). The constant need for capitalism to expand is the motor force that keeps the chicken dancing. There is no Keynesian solution to this.

Tim Jackson's *Prosperity without Growth* (2009:188) offers a detailed analysis of the contradictions of capitalism and ecology. 'To resist growth is to risk economic and social collapse. To pursue it relentlessly is to endanger the ecosystem on which we depend for long-term survival', he writes. So an ecological macro-economic solution would have to go beyond the 'green New Deal' that governments entertained after the credit crisis because, as Jackson rightly points out, Keynesian economics is designed to stimulate growth through industrial production and consumption. Putting capitalism on an ecological footing therefore requires considerable regulation of and changes in 'consumption, investment, labour employment and productivity growth' (Jackson 2009:176). It is difficult to see, though, how such a root-and-branch economic and social transformation is going to be initiated by liberal-parliamentary states.

The claim of ecological 'reflexive modernists' that *eco-friendly* practices are starting to make a difference needs to be put in the context of surplus-value. Giddens describes capitalism today as a 'runaway world' of mounting uncertainties conjuring fears of an 'unpredictable future'. Giddens recognises the challenge and is unusually pessimistic about the prospect of states, businesses and consumers to work together in mitigating the effects of climate change. He nonetheless favours a state and market coordinated action, arguing that 'where a price can be put on an environmental good without affronting other values, it should be done, since competition will then create increased efficiency whenever that good is exchanged' (Giddens 2009:5). The possibility of sustainable 'green' capitalism rests upon the claims that capitalism is a dynamic system with the potential to develop means for reducing carbon emissions in the areas of production and consumption. Capitalism with the help of the state has, by this reckoning, the capacity to repress its *jouissance* while also remaining profitable. Ulrich Beck (2010:264) sees a reflexive 'cosmopolitan' perspective on the environment as the possible answer:

> Those who think exclusively in national terms are the losers. Only those who learn to see the world through cosmopolitan eyes will be able to avoid the decline on the one hand, and, on the other, to discover, try out and acquire the new options and opportunities for power which could make a difference. The sense of emancipation and power that arises from overcoming national barriers is what could – potentially – awaken enthusiasm for a greening of modernity.

Business is under pressure to transform its methods of production while also supplying the goods and services that keep the system in motion. By branding themselves as 'green' or ecologically friendly, business is hostage to the charge of simply engaging in impression management. Airlines, car manufacturers and petroleum companies are particularly vulnerable to this criticism when the products and services they provide are essential to our current way of life but fundamentally polluting. It is stating the obvious to accuse a company like British Petroleum with its aggressive environmental branding campaigns of 'greenwashing'.

BP (2010), the 'progressive, responsible, innovative and performance driven' company, set itself an impossible challenge to market itself as 'beyond petroleum' and promoting a 'greener' petroleum. Websites, annual reports, advertisements and corporate brochures are carefully crafted to show its commitment to green issues. The panacea is consumption without consequences, exchange-value without the exploitation of use-values, coffee without the caffeine. BP can only produce platitudes: 'We help the world meet its growing need for heat, light and mobility, and strive to do so by producing energy that is affordable, secure and doesn't damage the environment.' (Cited in Boiter 2010) Global responsibility demands a global corporation helping the world to consume resources that inevitably cause global warming without damaging the environment or the reputation of companies that don the green clothing. There is no contradiction here according to Tony Hayward, BP's former chief executive:

I don't see a distinction between sustainability and performance. My aim for BP is that its performance should be sustainable – in other words everything we do each day should contribute in some way to the long-term health of BP and that of the environment and society. (Cited in BP plc 2009)

While fuels burn, the battle shifts to the margins where consumers can act in socially responsible ways by consuming from companies with environmental policies. BP graphically illustrates the problem. Its claims about sustainable practice are so easy to refute that criticisms of the company can in themselves act like a smokescreen for the all-too-apparent fact that companies are trapped in their own iron cage of surplus-value. In this respect, Lacan is right to claim that capitalists are exploited too by their own unobtainable object of desire. Described as the 'worst environmental disaster in history', the Deepwater Horizon oil-rig disaster illustrates the fix that companies are in. However culpable BP is, for every hole that is plugged there is another leak, hurricane, flood or forest fire waiting to happen. BP is only symptomatic of a more fundamental problem that cosmopolitanism is unable to resolve. I return to BP later.

Carbon Zero

What is really achieved in reducing our individual 'carbon footprints' when everything we depend on contributes to global warming? 'Environmentally friendly' practice confirms Marx's point about the fetishishised nature of the commodity. The sustainable solutions to global warming obscure the totality of the chain of production and the relations that lie within.

James Lovelock illustrates the hidden nature of the commodity in the case of wind turbines. He writes that construction of a one gigawatt wind farm would require 2 million tonnes of concrete 'sufficient to build a town for 100,000 people living in 30,000 homes; making use of that concrete would release about 1 million tons of carbon dioxide in the air.' (2009:17) On a daily basis, people ritualistically recycle bottles and cans and consume products purporting to be kind to the environment by acting as if there was no burning of fossil fuel at any stage in the production, distribution or exchange of the thing bought or recycled. The cynic knows this, shrugs her shoulders or entertains obscure beliefs that the discourse on climate change is a capitalist conspiracy designed to provoke fear in the masses. Those more respectful of science embrace enterprising abstractions such as carbon trading and see hope in technological innovations such as carbon neutral motorcars. We return to the same point of indeterminacy of cause, fetishisation of responsibility and enterprise as an ideology of pro-active political inaction. As Maniates writes:

> In our struggle to bridge the gap between our morals and our practices, we stay busy – but busy doing that with which we're most familiar and comfortable: consuming our way (we hope) to a better America and a better world. When confronted by environmental ills – ills many confess to

caring deeply about – Americans seem capable of understanding themselves only as consumers who must buy 'environmentally sound' products (and then recycle them), rather than as citizens who might come together and develop political muscle sufficient to alter institutional arrangements that drive a pervasive consumerism. (2001:37)

The individual consumer packs her gas-guzzling Sports Utility Vehicles with easy solutions to the global warming problem. Despite such contradictions, however, it appears that the 'individualised framing of environmentalism prevails, largely because it is continually reinforced' (Maniates 2001:41) – an indication of how socially embedded and hegemonised the post-politics of green consumption really is. Despite the fact that this collective obsession over green consumption choices and opportunities are in many respects meaningless, when it comes to tackling the key aspects of environmental degradation, the appeal of measuring our own ecological footprints on a daily basis is more about sustaining an ego-ideal than the ecosystem.

Global warming, while likely to impact on some societies more than others, has no territory and so monitoring and regulating the species has no boundaries; as a result, non-interventionist nation states become as impotent as individuals. There is currently a tussle between self-regulation and government regulation, voluntary and involuntary schemes for repressing individual behaviour. Agencies are called upon to credit our self-monitoring with symbolic ecological capital. New Zealand's carboNZero scheme is one of many that operate in this way.

New Zealand is more remote than any other industrialised nation. It has a low population density, a moderate to warm climate and plenty of rainfall to keep its soils fertile. The land, with all its unique flora and fauna, is the last place on earth for indulging fantasies of a simpler way of life – the ecological retreat of the last man. A highly neoliberalised economy, New Zealand also has one of the worst records on carbon emissions (Pearce 2009). Its environmental claims are 100% Pure New Zealand myth.

carboNZero was set up by Landcare research, a company specialising in providing 'solutions and advice for sustainable development and the management of land-based natural resources.' It describes as 'natural capital' the ecosystems that sustain the New Zealand way of life, the cultural aspirations of its people, and the industries and services upon which the New Zealand people depend. carboNZero is a certificate awarded to individuals and businesses that meet the following audited standards:

1. Understanding and measuring their greenhouse gas emissions.
2. Making a commitment to managing and reducing their emissions at source.
3. Offsetting or mitigating their remaining unavoidable emissions.

The carboNZero (2010a) site contains a 'travel & tourism calculator' to enable tourists to calculate and 'manage' the impact of their mode of transport, type of accommodation and tourist activity. The New Zealand economy heavily depends on international tourism and for such a remote destination long haul flights are unavoidable. It is the BP of nations, its entire brand a contradiction given what has to be consumed to get there. However, with the travel and tourism calculator we can at least marvel at the statistics. Going carbon neutral is indeed the mathematics of insanity; James Lovelock has a point when he writes,

> When I am warned that my pessimism discourages those who would improve their carbon footprint or do good works such as planting trees, I'm afraid I see such efforts as at best romantic nonsense, or at worst hypocrisy. Agencies now exist which allow air travelers to plant trees to offset the extra carbon dioxide their plane adds to the overburdened air. How like the indulgences once sold by the Catholic Church to wealthy sinners to offset the time they might otherwise spend in purgatory. (2009:18)

Becoming carbon neutral means never arriving at the point of being carbon neutral. It is an endless quest of filling in the ideological content in the lack of sustainable production through a process of practical enterprise. Carbon emission schemes such as these are found in every country to function as enterprising alternatives to the political actions that global warming necessitate.

With so little to sacrifice everyone can make a difference. The Nature.org site (2010) includes a top ten of energy and climate-saving tips,

> Walk or bike instead of driving a car. For office meetings, if you can telephone or videoconference, you will save time, money, and carbon emissions. Use compact fluorescent light bulbs. Recycle and use recycled products. Check your automobile monthly to ensure that the tires are fully inflated. Plant native trees. Turn down the heat or air conditioning when you leave the house or go to bed. Buy renewable energy. Shop at a local farmers market and you will find fresh and healthy foods, and help save our climate.

'The climate' much like 'the market' is the reified victim of our own excess. It is difficult to imagine anyone living such a regimented life. Not only are the suggestions implausible for most people, they would likely have no positive effect on 'saving the climate'. Yet this is what the climate change discourse amounts to; it encourages a self-governing and entirely impotent practice.

Technologies of governance are created to help us monitor our own behaviour. Their use is more affective than effective, symbolic rather than physical, brain rather than biology. The global warming industry produces an ideology for inaction. Consider, for example, the rugby player Conrad Smith, a local celebrity recipient of the carboNZero award. He writes,

> My job as a professional rugby player means that I fly frequently to different parts of the world. With that comes an environmental impact that, unfortunately, I cannot do a lot about. However, I am able to control other aspects of my personal environmental impact. (Cited in carboNZero 2010b)

The hegemonic ideology operates through a discourse that accepts the science and promulgates a politically neutral solution. For a planetary embedded capitalism the progressive solutions are left-liberal by default, constructing in the process an ethical injunction to act in enterprising ways to calm anxiety, fear and guilt. The performance principle is honed for end-capitalism with the subject as the happy consciousness satisfied that on the menu of carbon neutral options there is a healthy diet of growth and sustainability.

(M)Other Earth

In the Calvinist doctrine of predestination, the 'elect' could be identified by their material prosperity linked to hard work and enterprise. We can predict a different kind of 'elective affinity' between those advocating a return to a simpler way of life, essentially to remove the stain of human progress in the capitalist period, and the rise of authoritarianism in the west. As the effects of global warming begin to be felt on the economy, the calls for governmental action will help legitimate austerity, intervention abroad and repression at home.

The ideology on consumerism, which defines man as atom and society as individuation, organises into its lexicon words pertaining to the destructive effect of the species on the planet. Non-human species become our new victims and, when that ecological catastrophe finally happens, Gaia, like the terrorists who plotted the 9/11 attacks, would have had its revenge.

James Lovelock's (Lovelock & Margulis 1974) Gaia hypothesis popularised the idea that the biosphere is a self-regulating system in which all living species act together like a single entity. Unable to distinguish between capitalism and the species, Lovelock's (2009) solution to the imbalance that humans create is for a much-diminished global population to withdraw to small island enclaves, a chemotherapy for the planet. Yet the idea of Gaia as a single organism contradicts Darwinian evolutionary science, according to which organisms can only evolve by coming into contact and reacting with other organisms (Hird 2010). There is no other that earth comes into contact with. The dialectics of the enlightenment play out in this anti-Darwinian philosophy.

On one side there are commentators such as Daniel Gilbert (2006) who writes in the *Los Angeles Times* that,

> The human brain is a remarkable device that was designed to rise to special occasions. We are the progeny of people who hunted and gathered, whose

lives were brief and whose greatest threat was a man with a stick. When terrorists attack, we respond with crushing force and firm resolve, just as our ancestors would have. Global warming is a deadly threat precisely because it fails to trip the brain's alarm, leaving us soundly asleep in a burning bed.

On the other side there are figures such as John Zerzan (cited in Gowdy 1997:273), who cites Paleolithic hunter-gatherer societies as the ideal future of a 'disalienated' (from nature) human life,

> To 'define' a disalienated world would be impossible and even undesirable, but I think we can and should try to reveal the unworld of today and how it got this way. We have taken a monstrously wrong turn with symbolic culture and division of labour, from a place of enchantment, understanding, and wholeness to the absence we find at the heart of the doctrine of progress. Empty and emptying, the logic of domestication, with its demand to control everything, now shows us the ruin of civilisation that ruins the rest. Assuming the inferiority of nature enables the domination of cultural systems that soon will make the very earth uninhabitable.

The human species with its incessant drive to exceed mere life is imagined as inferior to the balance that animals arbitrarily sustain. With nature at stake, drastic action against the industrial base of society is justified by the counter culture of eco warriors such as Derrick Jensen (cited in Oleson 2007:88) who says,

> I think that twelve hackers could take down the electrical grid of all of North America, a blackout lasting for months. That blackout itself would take out key components [of civilisation]. Of course those in power would immediately start retooling, and because they have more resources than we do they'd eventually be able to come back online. We'd have to hit them again in the meantime.[2]

The Earth First! (2010) movement offers stark warnings and drastic solutions:

> The very future of life on Earth is in danger. The destruction of the Earth and its sustainable indigenous cultures has led to tragedy in every corner of the globe. On a more spiritual level, Earth Firsters understand that we can never be the healthy humans that we were meant to be in a world without wilderness, clean air and the howling of wolves under the moon. We

need to preserve it all, to recreate lost habitats and reintroduce extirpated predators. To put it simply, the Earth must come first.

Their argument for putting 'earth first' is based on scientific opinion. But progress for them means returning to a mythic past that involves wiping the dirt of industrial development from Earth's face. Mother Earth calls upon its warriors, the self-appointed Lorax's of Dr Seuss's fable, to speak for the trees, 'for the trees have no tongues', and to speak for the Brown Barbaloots who once played 'in the shade in their Barbaloot suits' (Seuss 1971). The founding slogan of Earth First! was 'No compromise in defense of mother earth!' Today they say, 'Together, we represent the voiceless wildlife' (Earth First! 2010).

When 'man' is conflated with capitalism, then it is the species itself that becomes incompatible with the ecosystem. It is not capitalism here that alienates man; rather that man in his species is the ontologically alienated renegade of nature. Overcoming alienation in this respect means returning to a mythical state prior to the ontological split of the species from the natural environment. 'De-alienated' man returns to his more natural condition, stripped of what distinguishes him as human, to become animal, not in the Deleuzian sense of exceeding one's molar identity, but a human without desire as the passive object of nature: a primitive communism where the 'i' of excess fades into memory.

Often accused of political conservatism, Christopher Lasch recognised the same anti-enlightenment thinking in what he called the 'party of Narcissus'. He writes,

Disparaging human inventiveness, which it associates only with destructive industrial technologies, it defines the overriding imperative of the present age as a return to nature. It ignores the more important need to restore the intermediate world of practical activity, which binds man to nature in the capacity of a loving caretaker and cultivator, not in a symbiotic union that simply denies the reality of man's separation from nature. (Lasch 1984:256)

The need to protect nature is greater than ever. However, by conflating capitalism with the human species, the tongue that nature is assigned is an unforgiving one. Beck is right when he argues that,

> If you see an opposition between modernity and nature, then you see the planet too fragile to support the hopes and dreams for a better world. And then you will have to envision and enforce a kind of international caste system in which the poor of the developing world are consigned to (energy) poverty in perpetuity. The politics of limits will be 'anti' – anti-immigration, anti-globalisation, anti-modern, anti-cosmopolitan and anti-growth. It will combine Malthusian environmentalism with Hobbesian conservatism. Beck (2010:263)

The problem with Beck's position is that the alternative he poses in no way addresses what is acknowledged as the 'indisputable facts portraying a bleak future for humanity'. If communism is unthinkable then the anti-politics Beck describes are inevitable.

The Elephant in the Room

The environment, Brockington writes, is mostly experienced at a distance. Adventures into the wilderness are 'infrequent, highly staged and carefully framed encounters provided by wildlife safaris or ecotourism trips.' (2008:53) The destruction of the ecology is symbolised in images of industrial waste and deforestation, but the hyper-real of global warming is symbolised in the city. Drawing on scientific data, Gwynne Dyer's *Climate Wars* (2010) constructs apocalyptic scenarios of cities and countries devastated by the effects of climate change. Hollywood ramps up the drama with films such as *The Day After Tomorrow* and *2012* (dir. Roland Emmerich 2004, 2009). In *Dead Cities*, written shortly after 9/11, Mike Davis (2002) notes the symmetry of fictional tales of destruction and subsequent real life events. The harbingers of the apocalypse may be onto something. For now, the big screen spectacle numbs and neutralises politics, providing entertainment and a frame to glamorise global warming for popular consumption. On the silver screen, celebrities indulge the wildest of fantasies, while on the small screen they campaign to preserve the wildernesses we never see, the species we never touch and the simpler ways of life so vulnerable to global warming yet so fetishised by our alienated eyes.

The invisible is made visible by the highly visual mediations of globalised environmental risks. They communicate local and global climatic events in highly selective, variable and symbolic ways creating a 'reality' that 'can be dramatised or minimalised, transformed or simply denied, according to the norms that decide what is known and what is not', argues Beck (2010:160).

George Lucas's *Star Wars* films were visual spectacles doubling as mass marketing campaigns for spin off products such as *Star Wars* action figures. The spectacles of global warming serve a similar function. Events such as floods, heatwaves, hurricanes and droughts are spectacular signifiers of the metacrisis of ecology, more hyper-real then real, with the culture of crisis industry providing the action figure equivalents to spellbound consumers. Baudrillard wrote in *Simulations and Simulacra* that,

> It is no longer a question of imitation, nor of repudiation, nor even of parody. It is rather a question of substituting signs of the real for the real itself; that is, an operation to deter every real process by its operational double, a metastable, programmatic, perfect descriptive machine which provides all the signs of the real and short-circuits all its vicissitudes... A hyperreal henceforth sheltered from the imaginary and from any distinction between the real and the imaginary, leaving room only for the orbital recurrence of models and the simulated generation of difference. (cited in Poster 2001:170)

The process towards hyperreality can be charted in global warming discourse. First, global warming was a pre-discursive Real. Long before the discourse on climate change, Marx warned about the effects of industrialisation on the soil: 'Exploitation and squandering of the vitality of the soil', he said, 'takes place of the conscious rational cultivation of the soil as external communal property, an inalienable condition for the existence and reproduction of a chain of successive generations of the human race.' (Cited in Harman, 2009:82) At this stage, then, global warming was prediscursive. Second, global warming was imagined. Science began to take note of global warming but there was insufficient evidence for making any conclusive claims. Third, global warming entered the symbolic realm, effectively where we are today with the climate change consensus functioning as a kind of big Other demanding carbon neutral consumption. Global warming also tarries with the hyperreal in visual representations of the likely impact of climate change. While causing local devastation, New Orleans (hurricane and flooding) and Melbourne (heatwave and forest fires) cannot match a visual imagination saturated with fantasies of the apocalypse in Hollywood cinema. The COCI helps codify the ecological crisis as depoliticised hyperreal. Only a 9/11-type climatic event has any prospect of puncturing a hole through it. The Deepwater Horizon disaster could never live up to such a billing.

BP sought to soften the image of petroleum by marketing itself as a pro-active sponsor of more sustainable practices. Its 2009 sustainability review (BP 2009) defines sustainability as 'the capacity to endure as a group: by renewing assets; creating and delivering better products and services that meet the evolving needs of society; attracting successive generations of employees; contributing to a sustainable environment; and retaining the trust and support of our customers, shareholders and the communities in which we operate.' There is nothing hidden here, sustainability by BP's own admission is about being profitable. It cannot be otherwise. Their 'programme of action' is composed of six strategies, 'efficient operations', 'efficient fuels and lubricants', 'low-carbon energy', 'assessing carbon costs', 'advocacy and outreach' and 'research programmes'. However shallow the sentiment, one thing BP is not doing, unlike its rival Exxonmobil, is campaigning against the science on global warming.[3] In this respect, the company is as progressive as any other on the issue.

In raising the profile of the environment at the petrol pump, BP made a connection between petroleum and pollution. By inserting the nozzle into the tank and pressing the trigger, the consumer discharged her guilt by association and got her piece of *jouissance* by providing a gift to 'Mother Earth'. BP and the customer were the partners in crime – one for extracting petroleum, the other for consuming it; by purchasing from a company concerned about the environment, though, a sort of confessional pact takes place, a confession of culpability and expression of willingness to atone for guilt by both parties. The Deepwater Horizon disaster undermined the symbolic efficacy of BP's green strategy by showing with blanket television coverage what we already knew about oil extraction. The disaster acts in the place of the little boy in the new clothes parable telling us to look at the disavowed place. The consumer becomes the victim of its own shallow commitments, reminded of the impossibility of a carbon neutral capitalism and now its culpability in being duped into consuming BP in the first place. Deepwater provoked a public anger against the tainted image of BP and the loss of a symbolic device that hitherto enabled consumers to purchase petroleum without feeling so guilty about it; retroactively, the *jouissance* recovered at the petrol pump was snatched back. Deepwater had the effect of demythologising green and revealing the hollowness of the consumer's contribution to the reduction of greenhouse emissions.

The Deepwater disaster makes us doubly guilty; guilty for consuming the product and for being duped into buying it in the first place. All our past sins rise to the surface, washing up against the shore of empty gestures with its resident collection of victims. Barack and Michelle's letterbox fills with our demands to punish the industrial miscreant; the state acts as the analyst into which the analysand's repressed memory transfers taking on the problem for us and then burying it in her own subconscious. 2007's Live Earth event was the culture industry's contribution.

2007's Live Earth was the 'monumental music event' for the mother of all crises, creating through entertainment the musical spin on the drama of global warming. It was a carnivalesque in absentia moment, more real than the reality of global warming, a medium without anything to mediate, end-capitalism's hyperreal. It was the ecological televisual equivalent of the 2003 global anti-war protests staged simultaneously in a number of cities including London, New York, Tokyo, Shanghai and Rio. Its '24 hours of music across 7 continents delivered a worldwide call to action and the solutions necessary to answer that call' (Live Earth 2007a).

The organisers had pitched their product well by appealing to business instinct. The Live Earth (2007b) website makes the pitch by advising business that by 'giving the audience what it wants, possibly stepping ahead of your competition, and the likelihood of attracting sponsors and media attention. You may also find some financial saving through reduced waste and energy costs'. As a demonstration of the politics of the possible, the Live Earth event led by example, reducing 'potential greenhouse gas emissions by hundreds of tons by holding events in daylight at outdoor venues' (Live Earth 2007b). A 'team of sustainability experts', including John Picard, the former member of Bill Clinton's 'Green White House task force', were called upon to 'follow the waste streams of this concert and cover their tracks with green sustainable offsets. All air travel for Live Earth will be offset with carbon credits' (Ecorazzi 2007). This preferred 'model of sustainability' of the COCI aims to do no harm to the capacity of business to generate profit and people to enjoy the spectacle.

On message, Al Gore, the self-appointed Lorax, took the Tokyo stage in holographic form with a reported 'expression of amazement' on his face at the size of the audience telling them and us at home to 'be sure to call on your leaders and elected officials' to make the kind of 'critical changes' in their lives. Those who turned up to the event and watched it on television were the heroes: 'This is what Live Earth is all about', Gore said (cited in Live Earth 2007c), 'And I ask you to ANSWER THE CALL!' In the 1960s Guy Debord (1983:9) wrote of the spectacle that it 'presents itself as a vast inaccessible reality that can never be questioned. Its sole message is: "What appears is good; what is good appears."' A society fed on the spectacle of global warming demands holograms.

Live Earth is another example of the enterprise, ethics and enjoyment configuration. The ethical point is diluted for the purposes of making money with good-time saccharin sprinkled on. Enterprise and enjoyment create the necessary distance for the scientific implications to be absorbed without provoking action to disrupt the show, manufacturing a collective consciousness that unites people in their non-antagonistic, diverse, blank ways.

Criticising Walter Benjamin for his optimistic view that cinema has the power to show people how they are being exploited, Adorno wrote,

> The notion of collective consciousness was invented only to divert attention from true objectivity and its correlate, alienated subjectivity. It is up to us to polarize and dissolve this 'consciousness' dialectically between society and singularities, and not to galvanize it as an imaginistic correlate of the commodity character. It should be a clear and sufficient warning that in a dreaming collective no differences remain between classes. (cited in Adorno, et al. 2007:113)

However, there was a widespread cynicism towards the event. In response to this, the executive producer of Live Earth, Kevin Wall, defended the event as an 'accelerator' designed 'to mobilise' people who are concerned about global warming. 'This is music with a lot of scientists,' Wall argued (cited in Gundersen 2007), and 'You're going to be asked to join us, to go online, where you'll see carbon calculators, pledges you can make and seemingly small changes that take you from awareness to action. People will start to talk green, buy green and vote green.'

On the Live Earth (2010) blog, one contributor typically writes,

> Hitting the highlights of all the Live Earth shows is like trying to condense world history on a napkin. Days later, Live Earth is still going strong. That makes perfect sense. After all, regardless of how stellar it was, it's not about the music. Live Earth is about pledging to combat climate change.

The global warming industry fits the problems it campaigns about onto a napkin that the undimensional consumer uses to wipe from her face the 'inconvenient truth' of the internal relations providing the meal. The symptoms of global warming are condensed to a limited number of issues that enterprise can act on, linking the problem to reductions in carbon footprints and the failure of governments, business and individuals to 'take climate change seriously'. Progress is then measured by standards that are purely ideological. The food the consumer fails to digest is what Žižek calls the 'background noise' of ideology, the 'obscenity of the barbarian violence which sustains the public face of law and order.' (2010:6) The entertainment industry ratchets up the drama to meet a constructed consumer demand for ecologically signified products. The configuration of enterprise, ethics and enjoyment ideologically triangulates end-capitalism, leaving at its centre the empty space that interpellates undimensional man as carbon neutral.

An event such as Live Earth is easy to dismiss as hollow spectacle and one would be forgiven for responding cynically towards it. However, its hollowness is hegemonic. There is nothing to do other than enjoy the spectacle of global warming. Within its ideological framing, the sceptic and the cynic are useful enemies to justify the publicity campaigns of the culture of crisis industry that saturates vision with spectacle at risk of bringing about its own crisis of overaccumulation of green signifiers. Enterprise answers to the criticism of interpassive enjoyment of global warming by the creation of events such as Live Earth. Attendance signifies passive activity. Entertainment as a form of surplus enjoyment creates the mass markets that capital needs to make profit from the crisis.

The entrepreneurialism of green business and the environmental gestures of consumers enter into an elective affinity with actual ecological crises and the entertainment industry. The 'tipping point' is when society is forced to acknowledge the elephant in the room and shoot it.

Earth Second!

> Labour... is a process in which both man and Nature participate, and in which man of his own accord starts, regulates, and controls the material reactions between himself and Nature. He opposes himself to Nature as one of her own forces, setting in motion arms and legs, head and hands, the natural forces of his body, in order to appropriate Nature's productions in the form adapted to his own wants. (Marx 2001:257)

As identity is intertwined with the consumed product, self-activity and self-fulfilment dissolve into the monetary footprint. The human is the alienated species of planetary nature and in his alienation from relations with his own kind becomes ensnared, in ancient tree roots and unyielding vineyards of the unforgiving effects of global warming; the 'trench-systems of modern warfare' (Gramsci 1971) are today the obscenities of the market and of the nature that the market threatens to unleash. Werner Herzog's description of the jungle reads as a deconstruction of the two:

> Nature here is vile and base. I would see fornication and asphyxiation and choking and fighting for survival and... growing and... just rotting away. Of course, there's a lot of misery. But it is the same misery that is all around us. The trees here are in misery, and the birds are in misery. I don't think they – they sing. They just screech in pain. It's like a curse weighing on an entire landscape. And whoever...goes too deep into this has his share of his curse. It is the harmony of... overwhelming and collective murder.
>
> Herzog, in *Burden of Dreams* (dir. Les Blank, 1982)

Capitalism has failed to tame nature, and now nature threatens the overwhelming and collective murder of the millions of people most vulnerable to the effects of global warming. The rotting of the species in symmetry to the fetishisation of nature reveals its spectacular force to global audiences. In *Against Nature*, J. K. Huysmans' fictional vehicle Des Essentes waxes another poetic deconstruction,

> Nature... has had her day; she has finally and utterly exhausted the patience of sensitive observers by the revolting uniformity of her landscapes and skyscapes. After all, what platitudinous limitations she imposes, like a tradesman specialising in a single line of business; what petty-minded restrictions, like a shopkeeper stocking one article to the exclusion of all others; what a monotonous store of meadows and trees, what a commonplace display of mountains and sea! (1959:36)

The superiority of human life is revealed in the artifices and excesses of art, science, love and politics, the four truth-domains identified by Badiou. And whether for our practical needs, aesthetic pleasures, perverse enjoyment or compassion for living things, it is in our collective interest to protect and preserve nature in all its obscenity so that human alien life can flourish. We are environmentalists by default. The political question, however, centres on what we are prepared to sacrifice in response to the threats that nature poses and ideology obscures.

As history has shown us, battles cannot be won when people are divided. The struggle against nature is first and foremost a struggle to overcome the structural antagonisms that leave us vulnerable to nature's more unified wrath. The apocalyptic scenarios forewarned in science and visualised in Hollywood cinema are the ones commissioned under capitalism. Global warming is a capitalist construct, written for viewers of end-capitalism who in their conscientious ways will always toss the tin can, out of which they quaffed *Cola-Cola Zero* or a fruitier local beverage containing vitamin C, into a recycling bin if there happens to be one in the vicinity. To denaturalise global warming, we first need to transform the forces and relations of production. Only then do we change our own socially determined nature and enact a metabolic balance of a kind. The left, however, would need to sidestep the discourse to bring into being an antagonistic subject that can potentially write the apocalypse out of the script. Only a unified humanity can respond to global warming without sacrificing either the excesses that define human life or the principle of universal equality and justice. It is no less rational to imagine the end of the world than to imagine a life without many of the pleasures and excesses that define human life. The struggle to preserve the environment for human habitation is foremost a struggle against capitalism.

Conclusion

The left-liberal solutions to global warming proposed by Giddens and Beck are unrealistic. The longer the politics of climate change is stuck in this kind of rendering, the more likely we are to get the authoritarian solutions Beck and Giddens warn of. The shock doctrine of disaster capitalism that Naomi Klein wrote about has the potential to go global. The crises spectacles feeding the culture of crisis industry prepares the ground for such an eventuality.

We can invoke one of the few genuinely but essentially marginal positive effects of environmental management to sum up the argument of the chapter. Due to the introduction of goats onto the islands of the Galapagos, the giant tortoise population had reached a species-endangering low of 15. Through successful management of the island, that number is now around 1500 (Carroll 2010). To achieve this, a goat was fitted with a tracking device and then left to naturally wander towards the missing herds thereby locating them for slaughter. Marxism is the tracking device that keeps locating the herd, but we need a political subject to do the dirty work of slaughtering it. There is no such agent within the climate change discourse.

7
CONCLUSION

Guy Debord said that 'The forces that have escaped us *display themselves* to us in all their power.' (1983:16) The naked effect of a system that survives by the expropriation of all human and environmental resources is there for all of us to see; the problem has been and still is that we weave, to be sure with the help of various agencies, an ideological clothing to suit our ragtag anxieties, fears, prejudices, cynicism and desire. As the Emperor charts his naked path through the corridors of parliament, the university, the corporation and every sinew of public life, we need the metaphorical boys and girls of the new clothes fable. More than this, we need another type of clothing, the clothing not only of compassion but also of belief. We need a belief that however unlikely it seems, a system that thrives on violence, inequality, alienation, cynicism and despair can be overcome.

Capitalism strips the dignity from women, the ground from immigrants and the power from workers. Its clothes are always new, and as it enters in ever more catastrophic crises we do ideological overtime to dress it up in ever more elaborate ways. In regard to Chapter 2 on the economy, this is not the time to be talking about mobilities, complexity and cosmopolitan futures. If we are guilty for anything it is in accepting the market logic of capitalism, rejecting any prospect of an alternative and basing this view on a non-dialectic reading of capitalism. As the quest for profit tears through the lives of those on the margins and travels inexorably across space it threatens all our livelihoods, homes, communities, cities, nations and eventually, in regard to Chapter 6 on the ecology, the ecosystem that all species depend on. These scenarios of end-capitalism need to be rewritten.

We can think of the dynamics of materialism, ideology and desire as instances of enterprise, ethics and enjoyment, each with its own dynamic, with its distinctive forms, effects – cultural, political, social and psychological – and consequences. In the examples of enterprise, ethics and enjoyment we encounter different ways that capitalism is clothed while also revealing in their dynamics the objective character of ideology today, particularly as the logics of the three enter into ever more crippling syntheses. There is, however, a dialectical character to these, through which we discover the rational foundation for hope. The injunctions of enterprise, ethics and enjoyment can be made to work against one another in the forms they take.

Chapter 3 centred on the enterprise of becoming employable, an endless task to discover and embody the characteristics of a subjectivity named by capital. An aesthetic of employability ideologically decentres the objective primacy of labour in our lives. Employability is the new work ethic; its language belongs to the other.

Chapter 4 centred on the ethics of left-liberalism, the culture industry that feeds on crises and helps depoliticise them for mass consumption. The cause is rendered indeterminate and the responsibility generalised through attempts by a combination of agencies, that I called a culture of crisis industry, to universalise guilt and fetishise it for the purposes of exchange.

Chapter 5 centred on enjoyment, how the workplace becomes a factory of enjoyment, politics is trivialised and the other suffers so that we can enjoy those carnivalesque moments in which generosity is mere spectacle. One-dimensional man, one-dimensional woman (Power 2009), one-dimensional society has reached its 'late' stage, going beyond what Marcuse had envisaged. The celebrity has entered the home and the home has been emptied of its content. The undimensional man wills nothing.

iCommunism was proposed as the psychic image of a society organised around the pleasure principle, the antithesis of austerity, oppression and asceticism that communism represents. In iCommunism there is the Deleuze of productive desire, the Adorno of negative dialectics and John Holloway's idea of *communising*, a permanence of anti-synthetic thought and practice – never beholden to what Deleuze called molar identities – that escape or take flight from the one-dimensionality and force a political identity onto undimensionality.

iCommunism is an idea and a practice but is hardly the basis for overcoming capitalism. The state, however weakened by its own retrenchments, remains the fulcrum of power. It is where law is made, money secured, power legitimised and class divisions managed. In the state apparatuses we find the architects and overseers of neo-liberalism, the monopoly of violence and the means to use that violence in coordinated ways to crush threats, whether from organised labour or from the many embryonic social movements so often regarded as the heirs of the proletarian struggle. The one thing that connects all of us is our relationship to the mode of production and so there is only one mask, the mask of the proletariat that unifies us. It is the power of the proletariat, whether in the guise of men, women, students (many of whom now have to work to pay for their studies), immigrants, Jews, Christians, Muslims, homosexuals, peasants or social activists to withdraw their labour and engage in forms of action that in combination would, as we saw in 1968, threaten the system. If lines of flight and non-identity are our callings, we should ensure they are grounded by a unified struggle with the power to crush the system that inhibits and transforms desire for its own logic. Capitalism is exploited by its own drives. Let us do it a favour and bring an end to that exploitation.

NOTES

2 Naked Economy

1. For example, Saad-Filho and Johnston (2005).
2. See Daniel Dorling's *Injustice* (2010), which includes a vast array of statistics on the social impact of neo-liberal policy in Britain and around the world.
3. The spectacular growth of finance capital can be traced in its contemporary iteration to the US. The Federal Reserve under Alan Greenspan used low interest rates to stimulate demand for credit as a way to compensate for the long-term decline in manufacturing profitability and wage incomes. Robert Brenner (2004) notes how manufacturing companies were able to borrow money for capital expenditure without the prospect for turning the investments into profit. An increase in personal borrowing stimulated an import boom, in part due to low exchange rates exacerbating an already burgeoning balance of payments deficit. During this period there was a precipitous increase in the value of financial assets. This happened for several reasons. Low interest rates were one factor helped by the role of the Federal Reserve in injecting equity into markets to prevent an economic downturn in the non-financial sector. Also, in violation of government regulations, the Federal Reserve allowed banks to store up large quantities of long-term bonds. This was to have its most visible impact when huge quantities of equity transferred to the housing market. As the paper value of housing increased the equity to mortgage debt ratio widened, enabling homeowners to access large amounts of this equity on their properties. Brenner observes that, 'If one ... takes into account cash-outs through home sales and second mortgages, as well as resident investment spending and purchases of home furnishings, housing and mortgage markets have accounted, in total, for no less than two-thirds of GDP growth between 2000 and the first half of 2003.' (2004:81) By massively inflating asset bubbles, Greenspan had helped to prevent a major US recession. What had in fact happened is that a paper economy had masked serious deficiencies in the real economy.
4. There is a substantial empirical literature supporting these points. Kevin Doogan's *New Capitalism?* (2009) is a particularly useful source of information.

5. See Cremin and Roberts (in press) for a more detailed discussion of this.
6. Yasheng Huang (2009) has written extensively on the weaknesses in the Chinese model, exposing flaws in orthodox assessments of the economy and identifying structural issues that are likely to impede future growth.
7. I would like to acknowledge Jai Bentley-Payne for our discussions on the need for an adequate term to describe the post-2008 period. Out of these discussions came the notion of end-capitalism.
8. See Žižek (2008b), and Adorno and Horkheimer (1997).

3   Naked Enterprise

1. See Burchell et al. (1991).
2. See Nikolas Rose on 'psy' technologies, which describes the role of expert knowledge in providing us with insights into the 'precise ways of inspecting oneself, accounting for oneself, and working upon oneself in order to realise one's potential, gain happiness and exercise one's autonomy.' (Rose 1998:17).
3. For further information and analysis, see Cremin (2005).
4. See Du Gay (1992:629).
5. See Heelas in Keat and Abercrombie (1992:98).
6. See Garrahan and Stewart (1992:98).
7. See Cremin (2003) for a summary of a content analysis that I conducted on situations vacant columns covering a 100-year period.
8. Aspects of this argument can also be found in Cremin (2010).
9. See McQuaid and Lindsay (2005) for a comprehensive range of definitions of the word.
10. The use of Lacan in organisational studies is fairly recent. Notable examples include Arnaud (2002), Böhm and De Cock (2005), Daly (1999), Fleming and Spicer (2003), Jones and Spicer (2005) and Roberts (2005).
11. See Lacan (1997).
12. See Armstrong (2001), Jones and Spicer (2005) and Ogbor (2000) on the entrepreneurial subject.
13. See Fink, 1997.
14. See Cremin (2003).
15. Not all firms operate according to this logic. But the mediating function of the employability discourse, and, in this respect, what obtains in the fantasy of the post-bureaucratic firm, is sustained in the practice of those seeking to improve their employment practice – as measured by the sheer quantity of career websites advising on managerial-style supply-side strategies.

16. This is the term Weber uses to describe a form of action based on an ethical conviction; the person's actions are determined by morally held principles and so are not rationalised according to perceptions of the likely outcomes.
17. See Cremin (2010) for a more detailed account of this.
18. See Holloway (1991) and O'Connor (1999).
19. The London Times *Times Best 100 Companies to Work For* list includes within their survey a 'Giving Back' rank determined according to 'How much Companies are thought by their staff to put back into society in general and the local community in particular'. However laudable the motives, the companies and individuals regularly featured on such lists are not by and large in the market of making the world a better place (see Chapter 4).
20. Basso (2003) refers to a range of data showing there is a trend beginning in the 1970s towards the increase in relative (intensity of labour) and absolute (length of working day) surplus-value.
21. See Callinicos (2006) and Thompson (2003) for useful critiques of their argument.
22. See Žižek (1999).
23. See Lacan (1998).

4 Naked Ethics

1. Kantian ethics are often identified with the moral discourses of left-oriented governments who use a kind of 'categorical imperative' to intervene in countries where basic civil liberties are denied. Zupančič (2003) appropriates Kant into a Lacanian ethics of the act, arguing that because our 'normal' actions are fundamentally pathological, the norm itself that the categorical imperative invokes is already excessive to the situation.
2. Honneth (1995) diagnoses three principal moral injuries or differentiations of disrespect: physical violence against the body, loss of dignity in the denial of full legal citizenship and the devaluation of personal achievements or forms of life-affecting self-esteem.
3. See Chapter 1 on the kinds of content I have in mind here.
4. For example, Latour (2007) (actor-network theory) and Urry (2005a, 2005b) (complexity theory).
5. Cremin and Roberts (in press) on left-liberalism.
6. Douzinas (2007).
7. See executive summary 'the art of inclusion' by Helen Jermyn (2004).
8. Projects of Anthony Gormley and Spencer Tunick are cases in point. Gormley's *Domain Field* involved lay public in a sculptural process of transmogrifying the human form into a life-size fractal skeleton.

Tunick invited a large public crowd to strip bare at the cultural sites of Newcastle upon Tyne and Gateshead. By emphasising their inclusive nature, such events earn the support of funding bodies and civic councils. They can be considered a success because of the significant numbers of the local population involved in them.

9. See Pratt (2007) for a discussion on the social justifications for arts funding.

10. Sargeant, et al. (2008:268).

11. Žižek (2008b:430) argues that in a world where antagonisms are flattened, Bill Gates becomes the 'greatest humanitarian fighting against poverty and diseases'. This index illustrates the point.

12. See Hallward's (2007) excellent book on Haiti.

13. We could say that the commodity fetishist acts as if there is nothing beneath the surface, a point Žižek (1989) makes. While the fetishist gets off on the fact that there is something/nothing beneath the surface, the cynic who recognises the complex of social relations beneath the commodity gets off on his or her knowledge of the fact. In this sense, as with Freud's fetishist, the cynic's knowledge of the missing thing in the symbolic narrative (the critical substance) is also disavowed in the lack of political response when all possible responses are themselves presupposed to be lacking. The false certainty of the cynic acts as the cover for the critical substance. It is the cynic as much as anyone who enjoys the 'shine'.

14. This form of profit-oriented corporate philanthropy has been called cause-related marketing. See, for example, Varadarajan and Menon (1988), and on (RED) specifically, see Richey and Ponte (2008).

15. HIV/AIDS is easy to depoliticise, so is a useful commodity for companies to campaign on.

5   Naked Enjoyment

1. See Zizek's 1999 article for the *London Review of Books* with a nice summary of this point.

2. This draws from McGowan's (2004) *The End of Dissatisfaction?*

3. See Larry Elliot (2010).

4. See Cremin (2007) for analysis of the way contingency is commodified in the 'gap year experience.'

5. Thanks to Jai Bentley-Payne for suggesting this term.

6. Thanks to Julie Lord for providing information on these shows.

7. As Wettergren (2009:8) notes, 'humorous protest lowers the risk of angry reactions. Fun is also a means to gain the trust of the general public, facilitating the reception of the message.'

8. For audience figures, money raised and so on, see http://en.wikipedia. org/wiki/Comic_Relief.
9. The sketch is available on YouTube at http://www.youtube.com/ watch?v=t1MpLM53pLE [accessed 14 May 2010].

6 Naked Ecology

1. The neutrality of the signifier 'climate change' belies the evidence from each of these reports that, whatever the local variations, global temperatures are rising. 'Global warming' seems to me to be a more appropriate term to use. However, for the purposes of the prose I shall use both terms interchangeably.
2. See Oleson (2007) who examines the legal ramifications of eco-terrorist justification for such acts.
3. On Exxonmobile's attempts to undermine the science on global warming, see http://www.greenpeace.org/usa/campaigns/global-warming-and-energy/exxon-secrets. (Accessed 10 May 2010).

BIBLIOGRAPHY

(RED), 2010. *The (RED) idea.* [Online] Available from: http://www. joinred.com/aboutred. [Accessed 5 June 2010].

Adorno, T., 2000. *Minima moralia: reflections on a damaged life.* London: Verso.

——, 2001. *The culture industry: selected essays on mass culture.* London: Routledge.

——, 2007. *Negative dialectics.* London: Continuum.

Adorno, T., and Horkheimer, M., 1997. *Dialectic of enlightenment: philosophical fragments* (original edition 1947). London: Verso.

Adorno, T., Benjamin, W., Bloch, E., Brecht, B. and Lukacs, G. (eds), 2007. *Aesthetics and politics.* London: Verso.

Ads of the World, 2010. *Renault Megane CC: Che Guevara.* [Poster advertisement]. JWT Cairo. Available from: http://adsoftheworld.com/ media/print/renault_megane_cc_che_guevara. [Accessed 9 May 2010].

Agamben, G., 1995. *Homo sacer: sovereign power and bare life.* Stanford: Stanford University Press.

Alessandri, P. and Haldane A., 2009. Banking on the State. In *Federal Reserve Bank of Chicago twelfth annual International Banking Conference on "The International Financial Crisis: Have the Rules of Finance Changed?"* 25 September 2009, Chicago.

Alliez, E., Colebrook, C., Hallward, P., Thoburn, N. and Gilbert, J., 2010. Deleuzian politics? A roundtable discussion. *New Formations,* 68(Spring):143–87.

Althusser, L., 2005. *For Marx.* London: Verso.

Amazon, 2010. *Charity single for the Haiti earthquake appeal "Everybody hurts".* [Online] Available from: http://www.amazon.co.uk/Charity-Single-Earthquake-Appeal-Everybody/dp/B0035LBM5I. [Accessed 2 April 2010].

Amnesty International, 2010. *Throw a party for human rights.* [Online] Available from: http://www.amnesty.org.uk/content. asp?CategoryID=10370. [Accessed 27 July 2010].

Armstrong, P., 2001. Science, enterprise and profit: Ideology in the knowledge driven economy. *Economy and Society,* 30(4):524–52.

Arnaud, G., 2002. The organization and the symbolic: organizational dynamics viewed from a Lacanian perspective. *Human Relations,* 55(6):691–716.

Arrighi, G., 1994. *The long twentieth century: money, power, and the origins of our times*. London: Verso.

——, 2009. The winding paths of capital. *New Left Review*, 56(March–April):61–94.

Bachelor, L., 2009. How to recover from losing your job. [Online] *Guardian*, 5 September. Available from: http://www.guardian.co.uk/money/2009/sep/05/recover-from-redundancy. [Accessed 17 January 2011].

Badiou, A. 2002. *Ethics: An essay on the understanding of evil*. London: Verso.

——, 2005. *Being and event*. London: Continuum.

——, 2007. *The century*. Cambridge: Polity Press.

——, 2008. *The meaning of Sarkosy*. London: Verso.

——, 2009. *Logics of worlds: being and event II*. London: Continuum.

——, 2010. *The communist hypothesis*. London: Verso.

Bakhtin, M., 1984. *Problems of Dostoevsky's poetics*. Translated and edited by C. Emerson. London: University of Minnesota Press.

Basso, P., 2003. *Modern times, ancient hours: working lives in the twenty-first century*. London: Verso.

Baudrillard, J., 1998. *The consumer society: myths and structures* (original edition 1970). London: Sage.

——, 2001. *Impossible exchange*. London: Verso.

Bauman, Z., 1991. *Modernity and the Holocaust*. Cambridge: Polity Press.

——, 1997. *Postmodernity and its discontents*. Cambridge: Polity Press.

——, 2005. *Work, consumerism and the new poor*. Berkshire: Open University Press.

——, 2006. *Liquid modernity*. Cambridge: Polity Press.

——, 2008. *Does ethics have a chance in a world of consumers*. London: Harvard University Press.

BBC, 2009a. *About red nose day*. [Online] Available from: http://www.bbc.co.uk/rednoseday/aboutrednoseday. [Accessed 5 May 2010].

——, 2009b. *Red nose day 2009 – thank you for helping us to change lives*. [Online] Available from: http://www.bbc.co.uk/rednoseday/index.shtml. [Accessed 5 May 2010].

BBC News, 2005a. *Full text of Tony Blair's speech*. [Online] Available from: http://news.bbc.co.uk/2/hi/uk_news/politics/4287370.stm. [Accessed 10 May 2010].

——, 2005b. *Millions rock to Live 8 message*. [Online] Available from: http://news.bbc.co.uk/2/hi/entertainment/4641999.stm. [Accessed 27 July 2010].

——, 2008. *Full text: Obama's victory speech*. [Online] Available from: http://news.bbc.co.uk/2/hi/americas/us_elections_2008/7710038.stm. [Accessed 2 April 2010].

Beck, U., 2000. *The brave new world of work*. Oxford: Polity Press.
——, 2006. *Power in the global age: a new global political economy*. Cambridge: Polity Press.
——, 2010. Climate for change. Or how to create a green modernity. *Theory, Culture & Society*, 27(2–3):254–66.
Beck, U. and Beck-Gernsheim, E., 2002. *Individualization*. London: Sage.
Becker, E. and Jahn, T., 1998. Growth or development. In R. Keil, D. Bell, P. Penz and L. Fawcett (eds). *Political ecology: global and local*. London: Routledge.
Bello, W., 2010. Will China save the world from depression? In M. Konings (ed.). *The great credit crash*. London: Verso.
Bhabha, H., Ferro, M. and Kacem, M. B., 2007. *The urgency of theory*. London: Carcanet.
Burden of Dreams, 1982. [Film] Directed by Les Blank. South America: Flower Films.
Böhm, S., and De Cock, C., 2005. Everything you wanted to know about Organisational Theory but... were afraid to ask Žižek. *Sociological Review*, 53(s1):279–91.
Boiter, J., 2010. *Advice to BP: Forget your brand image and concentrate on your brand's soul*. [Online] Fastcompany.com. Available from http://www.fastcompany.com/welcome.html?destination=http://www.fastcompany.com/1639407/advice-to-bp-forget-your-brand-image-concentrate-on-your-brand-soul. [Accessed 5 May 2010].
Boltanski, L., and Chiapello, E., 2007. *The new spirit of capitalism*. London: Verso.
Boron, A., 1999. A social theory for the 21st century? *Current Sociology*, 47(4):47–64.
Bourdieu, P., 2003. *Distinction: a social critique of the judgement of taste*. London: Routledge.
BP, 2009. *Sustainability review 2009*. [Online] Available from http://www.bp.com/liveassets/bp_internet/globalbp/STAGING/global_assets/e_s_assets/e_s_assets_2009/downloads_pdfs/bp_sustainability_review_2009.pdf . [Accessed 5 May 2010].
——, 2010. *The BP brand represents both what we so and what we aspire to do as an organisation*. [Website] Available from: www.bp.com/sectiongenericarticle.do?categoryId=9020655&contentId=7037996. [Accessed 5 May 2010].
BP plc, 2009. *BP sustainability review 2008 (Press release)*. [CSR wire] Available from: http://www.csrwire.com/press/press_release/22592-BP-Sustainability-Review-2008-. [Accessed 5 May 2010].
Brenner, R., 2004. New boom or new bubble? *New Left Review*, 25(January-February):57–100.
Brockington, D., 2008. Powerful environmentalisms: conservation, celebrity and capitalism. *Media, Culture & Society*, 30(4):551–68.

Brown, W., 2006. *Regulating aversion: tolerance in the age of identity and empire*. Oxford: Princeton University Press.

Burchell, G., Gordon, C. and Miller, P. (eds), 1991. *The Foucault effect: studies in governmentality*. Chicago: The University of Chicago Press.

Callinicos, A., 2006. *The resources of critique*. Cambridge: Polity Press.

——, 2007. Does capitalism need the state system? *Cambridge Review of International Affairs*, 20(4):533–49.

carboNZero, 2010a. *Individuals – what you can do*. [Online] Available from: http://www.carbonzero.co.nz/action/individuals.asp. [Accessed 5 May 2010].

——, 2010b. *Leaders' climate change challenge*. [Online] Available from: http://www.carbonzero.co.nz/members/leaders.asp. [Accessed 5 May 2010].

Career One Stop, 2011. [Website] Available from: http://www.careeronestop.org/ExploreCareers/SelfAssessments/WhyLearnAboutMe.aspx [Accessed 10 January 2010].

Carroll, R., 2010. Galápagos giant tortoise saved from extinction by breeding programme. [Online] *Guardian*. Available from: http://www.guardian.co.uk/environment/2010/jun/27/giant-tortoise-galapagos-saved-extinction. [Accessed 27 June 2010].

Casey, C., 1995. *Work, self and society: after industrialism*. London: Routledge.

Castells, M., 2002. *The internet galaxy: reflections on the internet, business, and society*. Oxford: Oxford University Press.

Chiesa, L., 2007. *Subjectivity and otherness: a philosophical reading of Lacan*. Cambridge, MA: MIT Press.

Christofer, K., 2010. With Greece, don't believe the fights. [Online] *Guardian*. Available from: http://www.guardian.co.uk/commentisfree/2010/may/04/greece-dont-believe-fights. [Accessed 7 May 2010].

Clarke, S., 1991. *Marx, marginalism and modern sociology: from Adam Smith to Max Weber*. London: MacMillan.

Clausen, R. and Clark, B., 2005. The metabolic right and marine ecology: an analysis of the ocean crisis within capitalist production. *Organization and Environment*, 18:422–44.

Clinton, W. J., and Bush, G. W., 2010. *Help Haiti build back better*. Clinton Bush Haiti Fund. [Online]. Available from: http://clintonbushhaitifund.org. [Accessed 1 March 2010].

Conservatives, 2010. *Set up a watch party*. [Website] Available from: http://www.conservatives.com/watchparties. [Accessed 1 August 2010].

Costea, B., Crump, N. and Holm, J., 2005. Dionysus at work? The ethos of play and the ethos of management. *Culture and Organisation*, 11(2):139–51.

Couldry, N., 2002. Playing for celebrity: Big brother as ritual event. *Television and New Media*, 3(3):283–93.

Covalence, 2010. *About*. [Online] Available from: http://www.covalence. ch/index.php/about-us. [Accessed 2 April 2010].

Credit Action, 2010. *Debt statistics*. [Online]. Available from: http:// www.creditaction.org.uk/debt-statistics.html. [Accessed 27 July 2010].

Cremin, C., 2003. Self-starters, can-doers and mobile phoneys. *Sociological Review*, 51(1):109–28.

——, 2005. Profiling the personal: configuration of teenage biographies to employment norms. *Sociology*, 39(2):315–32.

——, 2007. Living and really living: the gap year and the commodification of the contingent. *Ephemera: Theory and Politics in Organization*, 7(4):526–42.

——, 2010. Never employable enough: The (im)possibility of satisfying the boss's desire. *Organization*, 17(2):131–49.

——, (in press). The Social Logic of Late Capitalism: Guilt fetishism and the culture of crisis industry. *Cultural Sociology*, (accepted for publication 2010).

Cremin, C. and Roberts, J. M., (in press). Postmodern left-liberalism: Hardt and Negri and the disavowal of critique. *Critical Sociology*, (accepted for publication 2010).

Daly, G., 1999. Politics and the impossible: beyond psychoanalysis and deconstruction. *Theory, Culture & Society*, 16(4):75–98.

Davis, M., 2002. *Dead Cities*. New York: The New Press.

——, 2006. *Planet of slums*. London: Verso.

Dean, J., 2009. *Democracy and other neoliberal fantasies: communicative capitalism and left politics*. London: Duke University Press.

Debord, G., 1983. *Society of the spectacle*. London: Rebel Press.

Deleuze, G., 1992. Postscript on the societies of control. *October*, 59(Winter):3–7.

Deleuze, G. and Guattari F., 1986. *Kafka: toward a minor literature. Vol. 30, Theory and History of Literature*. Minneapolis: University of Minnesota Press.

——, 1987. *A thousand plateaus: capitalism and schizophrenia*. London: Continuum.

——, 2003. *Anti-oedipus*. London: Continuum.

Divine Chocolate. 2010. [cited 27 July 2010]. Available from http://www. divinechocolateshop.com.

Doogan, K., 2009. *New capitalism? The transformation of work*. Cambridge: Polity Press.

Dorling, D., (2010). *Injustice: why social inequality persists*. Bristol: Policy Press.

Douzinas, C., 2007. *Human rights and empire: the political philosophy of cosmopolitanism*. London: Routledge.

Du Gay, P., 1992. The cult(ure) of the customer. *Journal of Management Studies*, 29(5):615–33.

——, 1996. *Consumption and identity at work*. London: Sage Publications.

——, 2000. *In praise of bureaucracy*. London: Sage.

Dyer, G., 2010. *Climate wars: the fight for survival as the world overheats*. Oxford: Oneworld Publications.

Eagleton, T., 1992. *Walter Benjamin or towards a revolutionary criticism*. London: Verso.

Earth First, 2010. *No compromise in defense of mother earth*. [Online] Available from: http://www.earthfirstjournal.org/section.php?id=1 &PHPSESSID=613753dd841b20056b1788990813a592. [Accessed 9 January 2010].

eBay, 2010. *eBay for Charity Fee Credit Policy*. [Online] Available from: http://pages.ebay.co.uk/help/sell/GivingWorks-fee-policy.html. [Accessed 27 July 2010].

Ecorazzi, 2007. *Live Earth to be carbon neutral, model of sustainable entertainment*. [Blog] Available from: http://www.ecorazzi. com/2007/02/16/live-earth-to-be-carbon-neutral-model-of-sustaina-ble-entertainment/. [Accessed 5 May 2010].

Elliott, L., 2008. Up. Up. Up. Child poverty, pensioner poverty, inequality. [Online] *Guardian*, 11 June. Available from: http://www.guardian. co.uk/society/2008/jun/11/socialexclusion.children. [Accessed 27 July 2010].

——, 2010. The lunatics are back in charge of the economy and they want cuts, cuts, cuts. [Online] *Guardian*. Available from: www.guardian. co.uk/business/2010/jun/14/lunatics-economy-cuts-frankin-roosevelt. [Accessed 20 June 2010].

Engels, F., 2009. *The condition of the working class*. Oxford: Oxford University Press.

Ethisphere, 2010. 2009's 100 most influential people in business ethics. *Ethisphere*. [Online] Available from: http://ethisphere.com/2009s-100-most-influential-people-in-business-ethics. [Accessed 2 April 2010].

Fink, B., 1997. *The Lacanian subject: between language and jouissance*. Princeton: Princeton University Press.

Fleming, P., 2005. Workers' playtime? Boundaries and cynicism in a "Culture of Fun" program. *The Journal of Applied Behavioral Science*, 41(3):285–303.

Fleming, P., and Sewell, G., 2002. Looking for "the good soldier, Svejik": alternative modalities of resistance in the contemporary workplace. *Sociology*, 36:857–873.

Fleming, P. and Spicer, A., 2003. Working at a cynical distance: implications for power, subjectivity and resistance. *Organization*, 10(1):157–79.

Ford, K., 2010. *Volunteering Disney-style is fun, easy for families with young kids*. [Blog] 15 April. Available from: http://thedailydisney.com/blog/2010/04/volunteering-disney-style-was-fun-easy-for-families-with-young-kids/. [Accessed 29 July 2010].

Foster, J., 1997. The crisis of the earth: Marx's theory of ecological sustainability as a nature-imposed necessity for human production. *Organization and Environment* 10:278–295.

———, 1999. Marx's theory of metabolic rift: Classical foundations for environmental sociology. *American Journal of Sociology* 105:366–405.

———, 2000. *Marx's ecology: Materialism and nature*. New York: Monthly Review Press.

Foster, V., 1998. *Developing your employment skills*. Surrey: Trotman and Company Ltd.

Fraser, N., 2000. Rethinking recognition. *New Left Review* 3:107–20.

Freedman, H., 2009. The Careers blog. [Online] *Guardian*. Available from: www.guardian.co.uk/careers-blog/added-value-harry-freedman. [Accessed 17 January 2011].

Freud, S., 2003. *The uncanny*. London: Penguin.

Fun at Work Company, 2010a. *Big smile please!* [Website] Available from: http://www.funatwork.co.uk/Activities/Fun/Bigsmileplease.htm. [Accessed 13 May 2010].

———, 2010b. *Laughter workshop*. [Website] Available from: http://www.funatwork.co.uk/Activities/Fun/LaughterWorkshop.htm. [Accessed 13 May 2010].

———, 2010c. *New receptionist*. [Website] Available from: www.funatwork.co.uk/Activities/Fun/NewReceptionist.htm. [Accessed 12 May 2010].

Furedi, F., 2006. *Politics of fear: beyond left and right*. London: Continuum.

Garrahan, P., and Stewart, P., 1992. *The Nissan enigma: flexibility at work in a local economy*. London: Mansell.

Giddens, A., 1994. Living in a post-traditional society. In U. Beck, A. Giddens and S. Lash, eds. *Reflexive modernization: politics, tradition and aesthetics in the modern social order*. Cambridge: Polity Press.

———, 2003. *Runaway world: how globalisation is reshaping our lives*. London: Routledge.

———, 2009. *The politics of climate change*. Cambridge: Polity Press.

Gilbert, D., 2006. If only gay sex caused global warming. *L.A. Times*, 2 July.

Global Footprint Network, 2010. [Website] Available from: http://www.footprintnetwork.org/en/index.php/GFN/. [Accessed 5 August 2010].

Goffman, E., 1971. *The presentation of self in everyday life*. New York: Basic Books.

Goldenberg, S., 2010. Nearly half of Americans believe climate change threat is exaggerated. [Online] *Guardian*. Available from: http://www. guardian.co.uk/environment/2010/mar/11/americans-climate-change-threat. [Accessed 23 April 2010].

Gorz, A., 1999. *Reclaiming work: beyond the wage-based society*. Cambridge: Polity Press.

Gowdy, J., (ed.), 1997. *Limited wants, unlimited means: a reader on hunter-gatherer economics and the environment*. Washington DC: Island Press.

Gramsci, A., 1971. *Selections from prison notebooks*. New York: International Publishers.

Gundersen, E., 2007. Big show, big impact? Live Earth hopes so. [Online] *USA Today*, 5 July. Available from: http://www.usatoday.com/life/ music/news/2007-07-04-live-earth_N.htm. [Accessed 5 May 2010].

Habermas, J., 1987. *The theory of communicative action, vol. 2*. Boston: Beacon Press.

Hall, S., and Jefferson, T. (eds), 2006. *Resistance through rituals: youth subcultures in post-war Britain*. Second edition. New York: Routledge.

Hallward, P., 2007. *Damming the flood: Haiti, Aristide, and the politics of containment*. London: Verso.

Hansen, J. and Hansen, A., 2009s. *A letter to Obama*. [Online] *Guardian*, 1 January. Available from: http://www.guardian.co.uk/world/2009/ jan/01/letter-to-barack-obama. [Accessed 10 May 2010].

Hardt, M. and Negri, A., 2001. *Empire*. London: Harvard University Press.

——, 2005. *Multitude: war and democracy in the age of empire*. New York: Penguin Group.

——, 2009. *Commonwealth*. Massachusetts: Harvard University Press.

Harman, C., 2009. *Zombie capitalism: global crisis and the relevance of Marx*. London: Bookmarks Publications.

Hartmann, M. and Honneth, A., 2006. Paradoxes of capitalism. *Constellations*, 13(1):41–58.

Harvey, D., 2005a. *The new imperialism*. Oxford: Oxford University Press.

——, 2005b *A brief history of neoliberalism*. Oxford: Oxford University Press.

——, 2007. *The condition of postmodernity: an enquiry into the origins of cultural change*. Oxford: Blackwell Publishing.

——, 2010. *The enigma of capital*. London: Profile Books.

Hebdige, D., 2002. *Hiding in the light: on images and things*. London: Routledge.

Hilary, J., 2010. The arrogance of Saint Bob. [Online] *Guardian*, 5 April. Available from: www.guardian.co.uk/commentisfree/2010/apr/05/ geldof-arrogance-poverty-agenda-starsuckers [Accessed 5 April 2010].

Hird, M., 2010. Indifferent globality: Gaia, symbiosis and 'other worldliness'. *Theory, Culture & Society*, 27(2–3):54–72.

HM Revenue & Customs, 2010. *Giving to charity through Gift Aid*. [Online] Available from: http://www.hmrc.gov.uk/individuals/giving/gift-aid.htm. [Accessed 6 June 2010].

Hochschild, A., 2003. *The managed heart: the commercialization of human feeling* (original edition 1983). London: University of California Press.

Holloway, J., 2010. *Crack capitalism*. London: Pluto Press.

Holloway, W., 1991. *Work, society and organisational behaviour*. London: Sage.

Honneth, A., 1995. *The struggle for recognition: the moral grammar of social conflicts*. Cambridge: Polity Press.

Hopkins, T., 1985. *The official guide to success*. London: Panther Books.

Horkheimer, M. and Adorno, T., 2002. *Dialectic of enlightenment: philosophical fragments*. Chicago: Stanford University Press.

Huang, Y., 2009. *Capitalism with Chinese characteristics: entrepreneurship and the state*. New York: Cambridge University Press.

Hudson, M., 2010. Where is the world economy headed? [Online] *Counterpunch 2010*, 1–3 October. Available from: http://www.counterpunch.org/hudson10012010.html. [Accessed 5 October 2010].

Huizinga, J., 1992. *Homo ludens: a study of the play element in culture*. Boston: Beacon Press.

Huysmans, J., 1959. *Against nature*. London: Penguin.

IPCC, 2007. *IPCC fourth assessment report: climate change 2007*. [Online] Available from: http://www.ipcc.ch/publications_and_data/ar4/syr/en/spms2.html. [Accessed 1 August 2010].

Jackson, T. 2009. *Prosperity without growth: economics for a finite planet*. London: Earthscan.

Jameson, F., 1993. *Postmodernism or, the cultural logic of late capitalism*. London: Verso.

——, 1998. *The cultural turn: select writings on the postmodern, 1983–1998*. London: Verso.

——, 2003 Future city. *New Left Review*, 21:65–79.

Jermyn, H., 2004. The art of inclusion. *Arts Council England*. [Online] Available from http://www.artscouncil.org.uk/media/uploads/documents/publications/phpyAtV3b.pdf. [Accessed 27 July 2010].

JobWeb, 2010. *How you fit into the tight job market*. [Online] National Association of Colleges and Employers. Available from: www.jobweb.org. [Accessed 10 January 2010].

Jones, C., 2010. The subject supposed to recycle. *Philosophy Today*, 54(1):30–9.

Jones, C. and Spicer, A., 2005. The sublime object of entrepreneurship. *Organization*, 12(2):223–46.

Keat, R. and Abercrombie, N. (eds), 1992. *Enterprise culture*. London: Routledge.

Kimberly-Clark. 2010. *Kimberly-Clark corporations provides support to Haiti earthquake victims*. [Online]. Available from: http://investor. kimberly-clark.com/releasedetail.cfm?ReleaseID=439319. [Accessed 2 April 2010].

Klein, N., 2007. *The shock doctrine: the rise of disaster capitalism*. New York: Allen Lane.

Krechowiecka, I., 2002. *Guardian, rise – Careers supplement*, [online] 5 October. [Accessed 18 January 2011].

Kregel, J., 2009. Why don't the bailouts work? Design of a new financial system versus a return to normalcy. *Cambridge Journal of Economics*, 33:653–63.

Krippner, G., 2005. The financialization of the American economy. *Socio-Economic Review*, (3):173–208.

Lacan, J., 1997. *The seminar of Jacques Lacan, book III: the psychoses*. London: W. W. Norton & Company.

——, 1998. *On feminine sexuality, the limits of love and knowledge: The seminar of Jacques Lacan, book XX*. New York: W. W. Norton & Company.

——, 2004. *The four fundamental concepts of psycho-analysis*. London: Karnac.

——, 2007. *The seminar of Jacques Lacan, book xvii*. New York: W. W. Norton & Company.

Langman, L. and Ryan, M., 2009. Capitalism and the carnival character: the escape from reality. *Critical Sociology*, 35(4):471–92.

Lasch, C., 1984. *The minimal self: psychic survival in troubled times*. London: W. W. Norton & Company.

——, 1991. *The culture of narcissism: American life in an age of diminishing expectations* (original edition 1979). New York: W. W. Norton & Company.

Latour, B., 2007. *Reassembling the social: an introduction to actor-network-theory*. Oxford: Oxford University Press.

Lazzarato, M., 2008. Art, work and politics in disciplinary societies and societies of security. *Radical Philosophy*, May/June(149):26–32.

Live Earth. 2007a. *07.07.07*. [Website] Available from: http://liveearth. org/en/liveearth/070707. [Accessed 5 May 2010].

——, 2007b. *Green event guidelines*. [Online] Available from: http:// liveearth.org/docs/greenguidelines.pdf. [Accessed 5 May 2010].

——, 2007c. *Al Gore appears on Live Earth Tokyo stage as a hologram*. [Online]. Available from: http://liveearth.org/en/liveearthblog/al-gore-appears-on-live-earth-tokyo-stage-as-a-hologram. [Accessed 5 May 2010].

——, 2010. *Official live earth blog*. [Blog] Available from: http://liveearth. spaces.live.com. [Accessed 5 May 2010].

Lovelock, J., 2009. *The vanishing face of Gaia: a final warning*. London: Penguin.

Lovelock, J., and Margulis, L., 1974. Atmospheric homeostasis by and for the biosphere: the Gaia hypothesis. *Tellus*, XXVI(1–2):1–9.

MAC, 2010. *Viva Glam* [online]. Available from: http://www. maccosmetics.com/giving_back/vivaglam.tmpl. [Accessed 27 July 2010].

Make Poverty History, 2005. [Website] Available from: http://www. makepovertyhistory.org/edinburgh/. [Accessed 2 April 2010].

Maniates, M., 2001. Individualization: plant a tree, buy a bike, save the world? *Global Environmental Politics*, 1:31–52.

Marcuse, H., 2002. *One-dimensional man*. London: Routledge.

——, 2006. *Eros and civilisation*. London: Routledge.

Marx, K., 1973. *Grundrisse; Foundations of the critique of political economy (rough draft)*. London: New Left Review.

——, 1988. *Capital, vol. 1*. London: Pelican.

——, 2001. *Capital, vol. 1*. London: Penguin Books.

Marx, K., and F. Engels. 1989. *The German ideology*. London: Lawrence and Wishart.

McGowan, T., 2004. *The end of dissatisfaction? Jacques Lacan and the emerging society of enjoyment*. New York: State University of New York Press.

McGuigan, J., 2009. *Cool capitalism*. London: Pluto Press.

McQuaid, R. and Lindsay, C., 2005. The concept of employability. *Urban Studies*, 42(2):197–219.

Merton, R., 1968. *Social theory and social structure*. New York: Free Press.

Mészáros, I., 2005. *Marx's theory of alienation* (original edition 1970). London: Merlin Press.

——, 2010. *The structural crisis of capital*. New York: Monthly Review Press.

Microsoft, 2010. Microsoft unlimited potential. *Microsoft* [online]. Available from: http://www.microsoft.com/unlimitedpotential/ AboutUnlimitedPotential/UnlimitedPotential.mspx. [Accessed 1 March 2010].

Mol, A. and Buttel F., 2002. The environmental state under pressure: an introduction. In A. Mol and F. Buttel (eds). *The environmental state under pressure*. Oxford: Elsevier Science.

Mol, A. and Spaargaren G., 2002. Ecological modernisation and the environmental state. In A. Mol and F. Buttel (eds). *The environmental state under pressure*. Oxford: Elsevier Science.

Monbiot, G., 2010. Bogus and misdirected, yes. But the Tea Party has a lot to teach the left. [Online] *Guardian*, 14 June. Available from: http://www.guardian.co.uk/commentisfree/cifamerica/2010/jun/14/tea-party-has-lot-teach-left. [Accessed 15 June 2010].

Monster, 2010a. *How can I make my CV more effective?* [Online] Available from: http://career-advice.monster.co.uk/cvs-applications/cv-advice/how-can-i-make-my-cv-more-effective/article.aspx. [Accessed 10 January 2010].

——, 2010b. *Returning to work after a career break* [Online] Available from: http://content.monster.co.uk/13903_en-GB_p1.asp. [Accessed 27 July 2010].

Mooers, C., 2005. Multiculturalism and the fetishism of difference. *Socialist Studies*, 1(2):33–54.

Nietzsche, F., 2003. *The genealogy of morals*. New York: Dover Publications.

O'Connor, E., 1999. Minding the workers: The meaning of 'human' and 'human relations' in Elton Mayo. *Organization*, 6:223–46.

Ogbor, J., 2000. Mythicizing and reification in entrepreneurial discourse: Ideology-critique of entrepreneurial studies. *Journal of Management Studies*, 37(5):605–35.

Oleson, J., 2007. "Drowned world": Imperfect necessity and total cultural revolution. *Unbound*, 3(19).

Oreskes, N., 2004. Beyond the ivory tower: the scientific consensus on climate change. *Science*, 306(5702):1686.

Osborne, H., 2006. *Stern report: the key points*. [Online] *Guardian*, 30 October. Available from: http://www.guardian.co.uk/politics/2006/oct/30/economy.uk. [Accessed 23 April 2010].

Oxfam, 2010. *Making fun of a serious issue*. [Online] Available from: http://www.oxfam.org.uk/oxfam_in_action/impact/success_stories/kalma.html. [Accessed 1 August 2010].

Palma, J. G., 2009. The revenge of the market on the rentiers. Why neo-liberal reports of the end of history turned out to be premature. *Cambridge Journal of Economics*, 33(4):829–69.

Panitch, L. and Konings, M., 2009. Myths of neoliberal deregulation. *New Left Review*, 57(May–June):67–83.

Pannone, 2010. *Working with Pannone LLP*. [Online] Available from: http://www.pannone.com/recruitment.asp. [Accessed 27 July 2010].

Parker, M., 2000. *Organisational culture and identity*. London: Sage.

——, 2003. Introduction: ethics, politics and organizing. *Organization*, 10(2):187–203.

Pearce, F. 2009. New Zealand was a friend to Middle Earth, but it's no friend of the earth. [Online] *Guardian*. Available from: http://www.guardian.co.uk/environment/cif-green/2009/nov/12/new-zealand-greenwash. [Accessed 5 May 2010].

Peters, T., and Waterman, R., 1995. *In search of excellence: lessons from America's best-run companies*. London: Harper-Collins-Business.

Phillips, A. (ed.), 2006. *Sigmund Freud: The Penguin Freud reader*. London: Penguin Books.

Polanyi, K., 1957. *The great transformation*. Boston: Beacon Press.

Poster, M., (ed.), 2001. *Jean Baudrillard: selected writings*. Cambridge: Polity Press.

Postone, M., 2003. *Time, labor, and social domination: a reinterpretation of Marx's critical theory*. Cambridge: Cambridge University Press.

Power, N., 2009. *One dimensional woman*. London: Zero.

Pratt, A. (2007) The state of the cultural economy: the rise of the cultural economy and the challenges to cultural policy making. In A. P. Ribeiro (ed.). *The urgency of theory*. London: Carcanet, pp. 143–67.

Pravda Vodka Bar, 2010. *Join the Pravda lifestyle*. Available from: http://www.pravdavodkabar.com. [Website] [Accessed 9 May 2010].

Prospects, 2010. *The UK's official graduate careers website*. [Website] Available from: http://www.prospects.ac.uk/. [Accessed 7 July 2010].

Ranciere, J., 2009. *The emancipated spectator*. London: Verso.

Red Nose Day, 2009. *About red nose day*. [Website] Available from: http://www.rednoseday.com/about_rnd. [Accessed 5 May 2010].

——, 2010. *Partners*. [Website] Available from: http://www.rednoseday.com/partners. [Accessed 1 August 2010].

Richey, L., and Ponte, S., 2008. Better (RED)™ than dead? Celebrities, consumption and international aid. *Third World Quarterly*, 29(4):711–29.

Roberts, J., 2005. The power of the imaginary in disciplinary processes. *Organization*, 12(5):619–42.

Rojek, C., 2001. *Celebrity*. London: Reaktion Books.

Rose, N., 1998. *Inventing our selves: psychology, power, and personhood*. Cambridge: Cambridge University Press.

Rushe, D., 2007. Forget work, just have some fun. [Online] *The Sunday Star Times*, 16 September. Available from: http://business.timesonline.co.uk/tol/business/industry_sectors/technology/article2459581.ece. [Accessed 13 May 2010].

Saad-Filho, A. and Johnston, D. (eds), 2005. *Neoliberalism: a critical reader*. London: Pluto Press.

Sargeant, A., Ford, J. and Hudson, J., 2008. Charity brand personality: the relationship with giving behaviour. *Nonprofit and Voluntary Sector Quarterly*, 37(3):468–91.

Sayers, S., 2007. *Marxism and human nature*. London: Routledge.

Schnaiberg, A., Pellow, D. and Weinberg, A., 2002. The treadmill of production and the environmental state. In *The environmental state under pressure*, edited by A. Mol and F. Buttel. Oxford: Elsevier Science.

Sennett, R., 2002. *The fall of public man*. London: Faber and Faber.

——, 2006. *The culture of the new capitalism*. London: Yale University Press.

Seuss Geisel, T. (Dr Seuss) (1971) *The Lorax*. New York: Random House Books for Young Readers.

Skeggs, B., 2005. The making of class and gender through visualising moral subject formation. *Sociology*, 39(5):965–82.

Sloterdijk, P., 2008. *Critique of cynical reason*. London: Minnesota.

Softcat, 2010. [Website] Available from: http://www.softcat.com/home. [Accessed 1 August 2010].

Starbucks, 2010. Ethos Water fund. *Starbucks* [online]. Available from: www.starbucks.com/responsibility/community/ethos-water-fund and www.ethoswater.com. [Accessed 2 April 2010].

Starosta, G., 2008. The commodity-form and the dialectical method: on the structure of Marx's exposition in chapter 1 of Capital. *Science and Society*, 72(3):295–318.

Stiglitz, J., 2010. Reform the euro or bin it. [Online] *Guardian*, 5 May. Available from: http://www.guardian.co.uk/commentisfree/2010/may/05/reform-euro-or-bin-it-greece-germany. [Accessed 7 May 2010].

Sutton-Smith, B., 1997. *The ambiguity of play*. London: Harvard University Press.

Swyngedouw, E., 2010. Apocalypse forever?: Post-political populism and the spectre of climate change. *Theory, Culture & Society*, 27(2–3):213–32.

Tamkin, P. and Hillage, J., 1999. Employability and Employers: The missing piece of the jigsaw. In *IES Report 361*, November. Brighton: Institute for Employment Studies.

The world of Chinese: Language-culture-business. 2010.Available from http://www.theworldofchinese.com.

The Fun at Work Café, 2010. *How to kill workplace boredom without a gun*. [Online] Available from: http://www.fun-at-work.org. [Accessed 13 May 2010].

Guardian, 2010. *Jobs*. Available from: jobs.guardian.co.uk [Accessed 27 January 2010].

The Nature Conservancy, 2010. *Climate change: what you can do*. [Website] nature.org. Available from: http://www.nature.org/initiatives/climatechange/activities/art19630.html. [Accessed 4 August 2010].

The Team Building Directory, 2010. *Fun at work*. [cited 11 May 2010]. Available from http://www.innovativeteambuilding.co.uk/pages/contents/funatwork.htm

Therborn, G., 2008. *From Marxism to post-Marxism?* London: Verso.

Thompson, P., 2003. Disconnected capitalism: or why employers can't keep their side of the bargain. *Work, Employment and Society*, 17(2):359–78.

Thornton, S., 1995. *Club cultures: Music, media and subcultural capital.* Oxford: Polity Press.

TimeBank, 2010. Available from: http://www.timebank.org.uk. [Accessed 4 May 2010].

Times Online, 2010. Microsoft. [Online] *The Times*, 7 March. Available from: http://business.timesonline.co.uk/tol/business/career_and_jobs/best_100_companies/article7030335.ece. [Accessed 4 June 2010].

Tourism New Zealand, 2010. *100% pure New Zealand.* [Website] Available from http://www.tourismnewzealand.com/campaigns. [Accessed 5 May 2010].

Turner, G., 2008. *The credit crunch: housing bubbles, globalisation and the worldwide economic crisis.* London: Pluto.

Urry, J., 2005a. The complexities of the global. *Theory, Culture & Society* 22(5):235–54.

——, 2005b. *Global complexity.* Cambridge: Polity Press.

——, 2007. *Mobilities.* Cambridge: Polity Press.

van Ark, B., Inklaar, R., McGuckin, R. and Timmer, M., 2003. The employment effects of the 'new economy': A comparison of the European Union and the United States. *National Institute Economic Review*, 184:86–98.

Varadarajan, R. and Menon, A., 1988. Cause-related marketing: a coalignment of marketing strategy and corporate philanthropy. *The Journal of Marketing*, 52(3):58–74.

Virilio, P. 2007. *The original accident.* Cambridge: Polity.

Volosinov, V., 1973. *Marxism and the philosophy of language.* Harvard: Harvard University Press.

Wade, R., 2008. Financial Regime Change? *New Left Review*, 53(September–October):5–21.

Walmart, 2009. Remarks as prepared for Mike Duke, President and CEO of Walmart, Sustainability Milestone Meeting. [Online] *Walmart Corporate.* Available from: http://walmartstores.com/pressroom/news/9279.aspx. [Accessed 29 March 2010].

Weber, M., 2003. *The protestant ethic and the spirit of capitalism* (original edition 1905). New York: Dover Publications..

Westwood, R., 2004. Comic relief: Subversion and catharsis in organisational comedic theatre. *Organisation Studies*, 25(5):775–95.

Wettergren, A., 2009. Fun and laughter: Culture jamming and the emotional regime of late capitalism. *Social Movement Studies*, 8(1):1–15.

Whimster, S. (ed.), 2004. *The essential Weber: a reader.* London: Routledge.

Wikipedia, 2010. *Comic relief 2010.* Available from: http://en.wikipedia.org/wiki/Comic_Relief. [Accessed 1 August 2010].

Wintour, P., and Watt, N., 2009. Brown: I should have done more to prevent bank crisis. *Guardian* [online]. Available from: http://www.guardian.co.uk/politics/2009/mar/17/gordon-brown-recession-banking-regulation/print. [Accessed 6 April 2010].

Wolff, R. Moore, B. and Marcuse, H., 1969. *A critique of pure tolerance.* London: Jonathan Cape.

World Economic Forum, 2008. *Davos annual meeting 2008 – Bill Gates.* [online]. Available from: http://www.youtube.com/watch?v=Ql-Mtlx31e8. [Accessed 27 July 2010].

Wright Mills, C., 1951. *White collar: the American middle classes.* New York: Oxford University Press.

Year Out Group, 2010. [Website]. Available from http://www.yearoutgroup.org/. [Accessed 7 June 2010].

Žižek, S., 1989. *The sublime object of ideology.* London: Verso.

——, 1997. *The plague of fantasies.* London: Verso.

——, 1999. You may! *London Review of Books* (18 March).

——, 2000. *The ticklish subject: the absent centre of political ontology.* London: Verso.

——, 2001. *The fragile absolute – or why is the Christian legacy worth fighting for?* London: Verso.

——, 2002. *Welcome to the desert of the real.* London: Verso.

——, 2003. *The puppet and the dwarf: The perverse core of Christianity.* Cambridge, MA, and London: MIT Press.

——, 2006. *The parallax view.* Cambridge, MA: MIT Press.

——, 2008a. *In defense of lost causes.* London: Verso.

——, 2008b. *Violence.* London: Profile Books.

——, 2009. *First as tragedy, then as farce.* London: Verso.

——, 2010. *Living in the end times.* London: Verso.

Zupančič, A., 2003. *Ethics of the real: Kant and Lacan.* London: Verso.

INDEX

Compiled by Sue Carlton

Page numbers followed by n refer to endnotes